THE ARCHAEOLOGY OF

THE WELSH MARCHES

S.C.STANFORD

Revised second edition

For Colin, Claire and Anne, who spent
their holidays on the spoil heaps

from
The Old Farm House
1991

ACKNOWLEDGEMENTS

Most of the information summarized here has been obtained by others over many years, though I have sometimes given it a personal interpretation. Where this differs markedly from other views it should be clear in the discussion. My debt is great to the 1980 editors, Cherry Lavell, Eric Wood and Hilary Davies; and to my wife Yvonne. They removed many errors from the original edition; any new ones are my own doing. I have been grateful for the use or adaptation of illustrations by: W.A.Baker, G.C.Boon, the British Museum, J.D.Bu'Lock, the Cambrian Archaeological Association, M.O.Carver, G.Daniel, English Heritage, P.S.Gelling, W.F.Grimes, G.C.Guilbert, Hereford City Museums, Her Majesty's Stationery Office, M.J.T.Lewis, The National Museum of Wales, B.St.J.O'Neil, D.F.Petch, L.A.Probert, The Royal Commisssion on Historical Monuments (England), A.Saville, F.H.Thompson and G.S.G.Toms. To them all, and to the many friends on excavations and in extramural classes who have furthered my understanding of this region, I say a sincere thank-you which extends to Peter Bell for encouraging a second edition, and to the staff of Print Logic for realizing it.

This edition has been brought up-to-date, if only by brief reference, with most of the more significant discoveries and publications since 1980. The text has been condensed and some illustrations and preliminaries omitted to achieve this compact, economical version but the bibliography and index remain, with revisions. I hope no matter of substance has been lost.

First published 1980
by William Collins Sons & Co Ltd

This Second, Revised, Edition 1991
published by S.C.Stanford
The Old Farm House, Leinthall Starkes
Ludlow, Shropshire, SY8 2HP

ISBN 0 9503271 5 8

Printed in Hereford by Print Logic Ltd

PREFACE

This study would not have been undertaken had not Cherry Lavell and Eric Wood focused their enthusiasm for the idea upon me. I have tried to make it readable for newcomers, and useful to older hands, as an introduction to the evidence and as a forum for discussion. It is not planned as either guide-book or elementary text-book for I hope it will be read as an essay on the problems of community survival within the geographical and political limitations of the Welsh Marches.

Field and laboratory research is continuous and some of the conclusions adopted in the first edition are already obsolete or untenable. The same fate will surely befall some of the ideas in this version but there should be sufficient evidence to show that they have not been adopted lightly. There should be adequate notice of contrary arguments so that the reader does not feel cheated if other interpretations come to be preferred.

Boundaries

Most borderlands have somewhat uncertain boundaries. Here, the eastern boundary of the Welsh Marches is taken to lie along the plains of the lower Severn and Weaver, and the western one along the edge of the Welsh Massif; they take in Herefordshire, most of Shropshire and Gwent, west Cheshire and parts of Clwyd and Gloucestershire.

Although the coverage has generally been taken to county limits, sufficient latitude has been allowed to include sites beyond these that are essential elements of the Marches' pattern in particular periods. Thus for the eighth century AD our boundary sweeps through Powys to take in the whole of Offa's Dyke and related works. Some will be disappointed that adherence to the topographical and county boundary of southern Powys has left the chamber tombs around Talgarth beyond our close scrutiny; others that our medieval retreat from Offa's Dyke has left the castles of Hen Domen and Montgomery with only passing reference. The same need to avoid being drawn too deeply into Wales has left the Montgomeryshire and Clwydian hillforts outside our detailed study. The decision to leave aside the exciting discoveries and publications of the past decade in old Montgomeryshire was that much easier for knowing that The Archaeology of Montgomeryshire by C.J. Arnold (1990) now offers a comprehensive study of the county's archaeology into the Middle Ages.

Dating

Secure dates are scarce, particularly in the prehistoric periods where we rely mainly upon dates derived from the assay of radio-active carbon-14 in organic material from archaeological contexts. Such determinations involve statistical uncertainty so that for a date of 2000 ± 100 there is only a 2:1 chance of the correct date falling in the bracket 2100-1900 and a 19:1 chance of it lying between 2200 and 1800. There is always the possibility of incorrect recognition of the sample's context and often lack of information on the timber's age when it was used in the building or hearth it is thought to date.

Carbon-14 dates are conventionally quoted in terms of Libby's original estimation of the half-life of carbon-14 as 5568 + 30 years although a better half-life of 5730 + 40 has long been available. It emerged that carbon-14 dates do not agree with dendrochronological dates, established back to about 5000 BC, which derive from tree-ring counts on long-lived species like the bristle-cone pine and Douglas fir in America and oak in Europe. Clark's correction curve, reconciling the two systems, was used to quote dates in the original edition but has been superseded by the Stuiver/Pearson calibrations in what follows. There are still many uncertainties, in particular for the first millenium BC; and it must be remembered that for brevity the dates used here are given without the standard deviations. For a convenient index to the original data the reader is directed to the official journal Radiocarbon (Newhaven, Conn.) or, for determinations up to 1982, the C.B.A. Archaeological Site Index to Radiocarbon dates for Great Britain and Ireland. Uncorrected 'Libby' dates are quoted 'bc' and 'ad'; 'Clark' corrected dates 'BC' and 'AD', like ordinary calendar dates; and 'Stuiver/Pearson' dates 'cal BC' or 'cal AD'.

Index

Except for places quoted as examples of place-name types or church dedications, sites within the study area are in the index, most with their National Grid Reference. Save for many ecclesiastical and medieval settlement sites on pages 153-157, indexed sites are also mapped. The reference to the map, as to any other illustration of a place or object in the text, will be in the index. The main bibliographical entries appear in the site entries with author and date of publication; full details can be taken from the bibliography.

Where technical terms have been used they are explained in the text when first introduced and this reference can be found by looking up the first page reference following the term in the index.

CONTENTS

Illustrations are by the author unless
otherwise indicated.

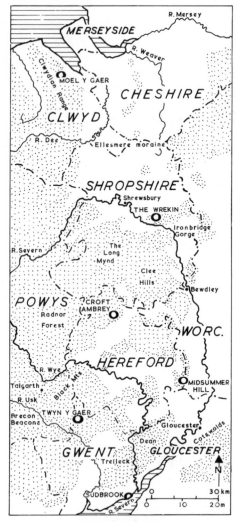

Fig 1 The Welsh Marches - counties,
relief and viewpoints. Land
over 122m stippled.

CHAPTER ONE

Viewpoints

The Welsh Marches is mainly a lowland area but the hills are ever present, whether close on either hand in the lower Wye valley or rising sentry-like on the horizon of the Shrewsbury Plain. It is never difficult to imagine the scout of a pioneering party climbing the nearest hill to survey the land ahead; nor to picture the folded terrain as the refuge of rebels during some oppressive occupation. It is easy to understand the attraction of the fat farmlands of Herefordshire to raiders from the bald uplands of Radnor Forest; and equally to see how the wealth of the Marches could support land-grabbing expeditions into neighbouring territories. From the six hillforts on fig 1 can be assessed the five regions of this study.

The Dean-Trelleck uplands (fig 2)

The southernmost region overlooks the narrow finger of the tidal Severn that brings in Atlantic influences, both climatic and cultural. The growing season here is long - eleven months with mean temperatures above 6°C at Usk, compared with only nine in Herefordshire at Ross-on-Wye and as few as eight in the central Marches at Church Stretton. The estuary narrows to five kilometres at Sudbrook Camp and at low tide is confined to the Shoots, a narrow passage between platforms of rock. Here is the lowest point for a short crossing.

In prehistoric times the Severn here was even narrower and this would have been the normal head of coastal navigation. Roman finds below three metres of estuarine clay on both sides of the channel attest to subsequent flooding which forced apart the communities of Somerset and Gwent, and buried earlier settlements under silt. With the drowning of the lower valleys of the Usk and Wye, the Severn now insinuates its saltiness deeply inland along their winding courses and leaves muddy banks bare as each tide ebbs. Between these rivers lies a wedge of coastal plain, the Caldicot Level, interrupted only at Sudbrook where a dry ridge runs down from the hills to the shore. On either side the plain has all the characteristics of reclaimed marshland, protected by extensive sea-walls against storm tides driven before south-westerly gales. Most of the larger villages find a dry foothold on the cultivable strip of Keuper Marl along the northern edge, presenting a glorious miscellany of Welsh and English names.

More decidedly Welsh in character and atmosphere are the uplands of Wentwood and Trelleck and the tributary valleys of the Usk: an irregularly dissected plateau where the Usk and Wye cut indifferently across geologically contrasting provinces. Since these hills only rise to about 200-250 metres there are some extensive cultivated areas but the frequency of steep slopes in Old Red Sandstone and Carboniferous Limestone has led to large areas remaining forested.

West of the Usk the South Wales moorlands shield the coal valleys from our view. The foothills are tracked by the Monmouthshire

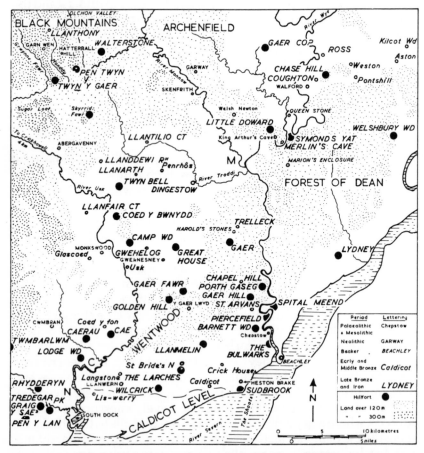

Fig 2 Selected prehistoric sites in the southern Marches. M-Monmouth, N-Newport. C-Caerleon

and Brecon Canal, in the wake of which have come the railways, roads, housing estates and glass-fronted factories of industrial Gwent.

The Carboniferous Limestone of Trelleck is separated from its continuation in the Forest of Dean by the deep gorge of the Wye. On the English side too the cultivated plateau changes abruptly to forest where the Coal Measures outcrop. The poor soils on the sandstones of the latter formation, the relics of centuries of ironworking and coalmining, the acres of sessile oak woods and the distinctive rural scene of smallholdings with outbuildings of iron-stained sandstone, combine to make the Forest distinct and isolated. Offa's Dyke and the later English boundary used the Wye valley to separate east from west; and the broken terrain and sparse settlement have continued to make the Forest a no man's land. Between these plateaus the twisting gorge is often too narrow to take a road as well as the river Wye; and the other major river, the Usk, is too shallow above Caerleon to have encouraged development.

The Herefordshire basin (fig 2, fig 3)

Through the hills between southern Gwent and central Herefordshire flows the Monnow, a tumbling stream of no navigational potential, that rises in the Black Mountains. Here, high above the Afon Honddu

Plate 1 The view east from the gate of Twyn y Gaer, Cwmyoy

and 426 metres above sea-level, is the hillfort of Twyn y Gaer, Cwmyoy, above valleys with chequered fields of hay separated by heather-covered ridges which deny communication with the Brecon lowlands to the west. As a result the Black Mountains have acted as a breakwater diverting the movement of people and ideas. They narrow and emphasize the Talgarth route into Herefordshire and give the Usk a role independent of the Wye.

The north-eastern ridges of the Black Mountains are lower and very much like the Old Red Sandstone uplands east of Twyn y Gaer, where the pasture is frequently interrupted by woodland (pl 1). In antiquity this south Herefordshire district of Archenfield was Welsh and place-names like Llangarron and Llanrothal survive.

Beyond Archenfield and the Wye rise the Woolhope hills, bringing up Silurian limestone near the very centre of the Herefordshire basin. The sky-line is held by the Malverns, fifty kilometres away on the far side of the Marches. We see how open northern Gwent is to attack from the English lowlands to the north-east.

Plate 2   The Malvern Hills looking south towards the Hereford-shire Beacon hillfort, crowned by its medieval ring-work, with Midsummer Hill Camp beyond

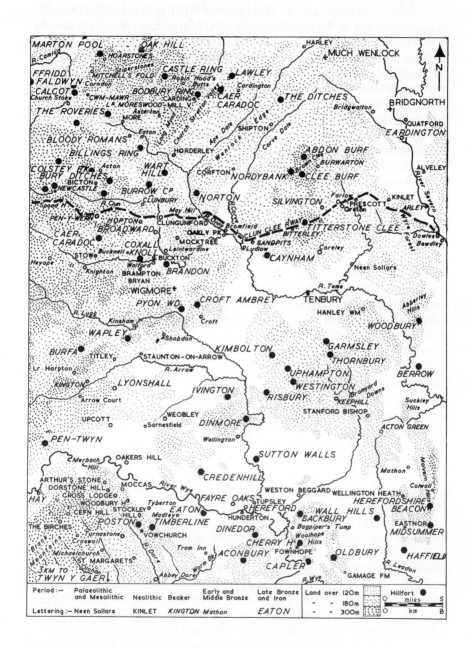

Fig 3 Selected prehistoric locations in the central Marches

When we move east to Midsummer Hill (fig 3) we stand on rocks as ancient as any in the world, causing the Malverns to stand up steeply from the Midland plain like the knuckles of a clenched fist to form a striking topographical and cultural divide (pl 2). The clay lowlands of the Midlands lie to the east. In the distance, trending south-westwards, are the Cotswolds, a level horizon of Jurassic limestone, 300 metres above sea-level, describing a geological uniformity on a scale unknown in the broken terrain of the Marches. Below them glints the tidal Severn passing Gloucester. In the north foreground is the Herefordshire Beacon, or British Camp, hillfort. Beyond that, along the west bank of the Severn, rise successively the Suckley Hills, Bromyard Downs and Abberley Hills. This eastern margin of the Marches is steeply accidented, with deeply incised valleys plunging to the Severn.

Westwards, in mid-Herefordshire, the upper layers of Old Red Sandstone have been widely eroded and the residual table-lands like Credenhill and Dinmore Hill have steep forested edges. Between such hills, which give a local relief of 60-180 metres, there are broad lowlands strewn with glacial drift. Outwash sands and gravels offer areas of lighter soil but there are regions in the west where drainage is impeded and there are pro-glacial ponds in the north between Staunton-on-Arrow and Shobdon. Nevertheless, this is generally regarded as rich farming land.

The central Marches (fig 3)

From the ramparts of Croft Ambrey, nearly 300 metres above sea-level, the Herefordshire basin lies displayed to the south. In fair weather the Black Mountains, Brecon Beacons, Forest of Dean, Malverns and Cotswolds can all be seen and the unity of Herefordshire is obvious.

South-westwards from our vantage point the wooded Silurian limestone escarpment merges with the hills of Wales beyond Kington. North-eastwards it curves to approach Ludlow, only to turn west again as Bringewood Chase before resuming its north-easterly course as the wooded front of Wenlock Edge. The geological regularity of this escarpment is succeeded north-west of Croft Ambrey by a jumble of hills which extend in limestone, sandstone and shale to the Camlad and upper Onny. There are many hills up to 275 metres but cultivation has surmounted most of them. They offer a tidy aspect of improved grassland between neat hedges, interrupted by patches of woodland with broader forests on the more extensive slopes (pl 3).

Roman scouts probed westwards through these hills against resistant Britons; and in medieval times the armies of Owen Glyndwr swept through to ravage the English. At Mortimer's Cross, where the Lugg breaks out of the hills, the Mortimers fought Edward of York for the throne of England.

At about the same latitude eastwards are the Clee Hills, of Old Red Sandstone capped by Coal Measures and basalt, with a considerable area of uncultivated land above 275 metres. A dissected plateau extends eastwards to overlook the Severn between Wyre Forest and Bridgnorth. To the north, between the Clees and Wenlock Edge, lies fertile Corve Dale.

North-west of Wenlock Edge are the ancient hills of Caer Caradoc, the Long Mynd, Corndon, the Stiperstones, Earl's Hill and the Breidden. For the first time since leaving the Black Mountains we have come into a region with large areas of limited agricultural value; but it possesses mineral resources that attracted prehistoric stone axe-makers to Corndon Hill and Roman miners to the neighbouring Shelve district. There, the abandoned pit-head gear of the nineteenth century lies awkwardly beside sacred prehistoric stone circles. We should ponder the grandeur of such hills for early people who lived so close to the land: 'The Crags of Caer Caradoc, Church Stretton' rise precipitously to 460 metres, and clouds often envelop the Long Mynd.

Plate 3 The south Shropshire hills east from Caer Caradoc hillfort, Clun

Plate 4 The Wrekin from the south-west

These hills extend the uplands of Wales across the border by way of Titterstone Clee to the very banks of the Severn, effectively separating the basins of Hereford and Shrewsbury. The Church Stretton valley offers the only easy way through and along it went the Roman road to Viroconium and later the railway heading for Shrewsbury. Southwards, the Romans entered Herefordshire by way of Leintwardine; the English preference for the Ludlow route was confirmed by the choice of that town in 1502 for the seat of the Court of the Marches.

The Shrewsbury plain (fig 4)

At the south-east corner of the plain of Shrewsbury is the rhyolitic hump of the Wrekin (pl 4). From its arched spine, within the hillfort

Fig 4 Selected prehistoric locations in the northern Marches
PYC-Penycloddiau; MYG-Moel y Gaer, Bodfari

Period:-	Neolithic	Beaker	Early and Middle Bronze	Late Bronze and Iron	Land over 120m		Hillfort
Lettering:-	LEIGHTON	*BROMPTON*	Battlefield	WREKIN	180m 300m		

the view south-eastwards is across undulating ground towards the skyscrapers of modern Wolverhampton. The Severn pours that way through the Ironbridge gorge. To the south and south-west stand the hills of south Shropshire: the clean sweep of Wenlock Edge, the volcanic protrusion of Caer Caradoc and the flat summit of the Long Mynd. Westward rises Moel y Golfa and the Breidden, embraced by the curve of the Severn as it emerges from mid-Wales to leave the greater part of the Shrewsbury plain north of its meandering circuit. Diverted from its Irish Sea outlet during the last glaciation, the middle Severn flows uncertainly over an uneven morainic surface. The area is generally poorly drained but has some more amenable spreads of gravel and sand. There are occasional sharply sculptured hills along the Keuper Sandstone outcrop at Oliver's Point, Grinshill, and Hopley Hill, and rounded knolls of igneous rock near Haughmond; none rise more than 75 metres above the plain.

The glacial debris of the Ellesmere moraine separates the Severn and Dee basins along a zone of poor drainage where peat bogs like Whixall Moss and Whattall Moss developed later : a land of limited opportunity, attracting fewer people.

The valleys of the Dee and Weaver (fig 4)

Near Mold, at the north-west limit of the Marches, a small limestone hummock is occupied by the hillfort of Moel y Gaer. A land of low relief, smothered by boulder clay and very green, extends eastwards to the low sandstone ridge that runs north-south between the Dee and Weaver. To the north lies the Dee estuary and the coastal route to north Wales. To the west, from Ruabon to Holywell, is broken country on Coal Measures and Millstone Grit. Behind is the Clwydian Range of Carboniferous Limestone, 300 metres high. Few roads cross it but it can be outflanked by the coastal route or the upper Dee valley towards Cardigan Bay or Gwynedd. The northern Marches were exposed to western intruders but have also served as a base for the invasion of Wales.

The physical boundaries of these five regions were mostly used for the historic counties (fig 1); and the physical divisions coincide with climatic regimes. Warm Atlantic air gives Gwent and Hereford a mild climate with lower rainfall than normal for western districts. But north of Ludlow the winter rain often turns to sleet and frost lies longer. Greater exposure to the north-westerlies increases cloud and rain so there is more grass in the north, more arable in the south; but north or south the Marches are fertile compared with Wales.

CHAPTER TWO

Palaeolithic hunters and
their descendants

The Welsh Marches, being distant from the chalk outcrop that offered
the main supply of flint, and close to the ultimate edge of the continent,
stood remote from the mainstream of man's Palaeolithic endeavours in
Europe as represented in the gravels of the Somme or, much later, in the
caves of the Dordogne. Indeed, it is only in Upper Palaeolithic times
26,000-8000 bc,* that the Marches has adequate evidence of activity
before the beginning of farming. There are also geological reasons why
the signs of early man in the Welsh Marches are so thin. North of the
Thames-Severn line the last British glaciation, the Devensian, overrode
the drift deposits containing Lower and Middle Palaeolithic implements and either scraped them away or smothered them with moraine.
So there is little chance of such tools being found on open sites north
and west of the ice front, which lay approximately along the line
Abergavenny - Hereford - Wenlock Edge - Bridgnorth. The Black
Mountains, Caer Caradoc, the Long Mynd, Long Mountain and a few
others would have protruded above the glaciers; but this final advance
buried the western plains of Herefordshire beneath more than 200
metres of ice so that hills 300 metres high, like Merbach Hill near Hay,
were overridden; and boulder clay was deposited at over 400 metres on
the flanks of the Wrekin.

In front of the ice, sand and gravel spread in the valleys of the
lower Usk, middle Wye, middle Teme and Severn below Bridgnorth.
From between Bewdley and Gloucester have come five Lower
Palaeolithic handaxes and an equal number of flake implements; and
from the Severn estuary Levels, three handaxes and a Levalloisian
flake. But to north and west, there is little of Lower or Middle
Palaeolithic date, covering more than 200,000 years of man's occupation of Britain, until Pontnewydd Cave is reached near Denbigh.
South-east of the ice front there is an ovate axe from Welsh Newton, a
Levalloisian flake from Chepstow and a handaxe from Neen Sollars,
east Shropshire. From behind the ice front at Sarnesfield, west Herefordshire, a handaxe and an Upper Palaeolithic blade are reported.

Homo sapiens sapiens, emerging as a distinct species by 35,000 or
40,000 bc *, occupied north-west Europe in the final phase of the last

* The use of 'bc' and 'cal BC' is explained in the preface

Plate 5 The Wye gorge from Seven Sisters' rock near King Arthur's cave

glaciation. He brought with him a new technique for converting nodules of flint into tools, preparing a core to allow narrow blades to be struck from it. These served, when trimmed, as knives, arrowheads, scrapers and points (fig 5, 1-8). This economical use of material made it easier to escape from the trammels of the chalk and explore distant regions; Upper Palaeolithic hunters could now exploit Wales and the Pennines. Large tracts of Britain were still under ice so it is likely that many of the finds reflect summer visits to the tundra on its edge. When winter froze the land again the animals retreated south, followed by the hunters. England was joined to the Continent and the estuary of the Severn was but a broad valley of a major river. Migration could have taken place freely over hundreds of miles but there may have been long periods when an ice retreat allowed hunters to establish themselves permanently on the edge of the forest or in the shelter of caves. From such comfortable quarters they might have organized at their comparative leisure the hunting of animals like the mammoth, with three young, whose skeletons, dated about 11,000 bc, were found in a sand pit at Condover in 1987. When the herds of mammoth and reindeer migrated there would have been wildfowl to snare along numerous streams and ponds.

We have little information about open-air sites. Instead, almost

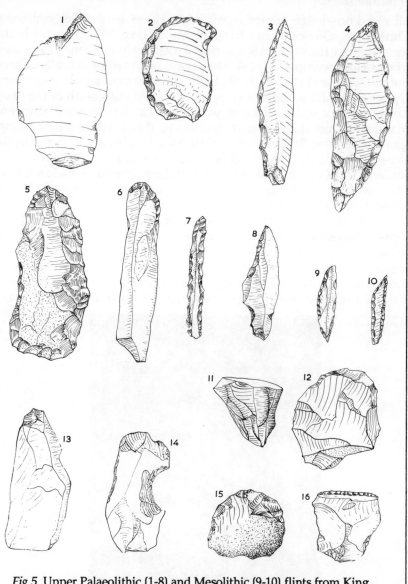

Fig 5 Upper Palaeolithic (1-8) and Mesolithic (9-10) flints from King
Arthur's Cave (after Taylor 1927); and Mesolithic-type flints from
east Shropshire (11-16, after Saville 1974). All 1/1

1 Graver   7 & 8 Microlithic points 11 & 12 Cores from microlith
2,6,15 & 16 Scrapers   9 Crescentic microlith   production
3 & 4 Points   10 Triangular microlith 13 Burin   14 Notched flake
5 Slug knife

all our knowledge comes from a few caves in the Carboniferous Limestone. One of them - King Arthur's Cave, Whitchurch - is 100 metres above the Wye (pl 5) and near a rock-shelter that may have been a Palaeolithic camp-site (pl 6). The cave deposits were virtually cleared out in 1870-1 and 1925-7 (fig 6). In the passage a cave earth containing Upper Palaeolithic flints overlay a hearth. At the mouth of the cave, under a recent stalactitic layer, was a cave earth with late Pleistocene mammal bones, then a hearth, and below this a red sand containing igneous pebbles. Symonds thought the sand had been deposited by the Wye flowing at this level but it could have come from above by an underground stream. Below this was stalagmite and then a lower cave earth with bones of cave lion, woolly rhinoceros, mammoth, hyena, horse, bison, the great Irish deer and reindeer.

On the platform the humus overlay a hearth with modified Upper Palaeolithic flints, perhaps representing a local Palaeolithic group surviving in a post-glacial environment. This occupation was separated from an earlier one by a layer of rubble over a cave earth with a late glacial fauna, including a giant deer, horse and bison, and Upper Palaeolithic flints. Below the second hearth was a thin layer with many

Plate 6 A rock shelter near King Arthur's cave, Whitchurch

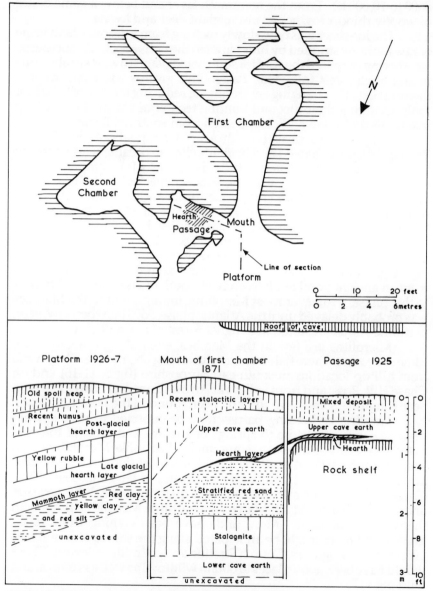

Fig 6   King Arthur's Cave: plan and schematic section, based on Taylor 1927

mammoth bones indicative of a glacial phase and in line with the
expectation that the overlying Creswellian occupation dates around

8000 to 10,000 bc. From the mammoth layer and below it came bones of woolly rhinoceros, horse, bison, giant deer and hyena.

The ice-sheet was now slowly melting from a desolate landscape of raw moraine studded by hills pared to the native rock. As sub-aerial weathering prepared the way for soil-rooted plants, dwarf shrubs came in and birch forest followed. Palaeolithic groups will have adapted themselves to the changing environment, reducing the size of their flint tools, changing their diet and hunting techniques as the herds of big mammals dwindled and disappeared from southern Britain.

The pre-Boreal phase brought a rapid change about 8300-7500 bc. The last of the ice thawed and Britain's climate became warm and dry with persistent south-eastern winds giving mean July temperatures of the same order as we enjoy today. Pioneer species like willow, aspen and birch quickly invaded the former tundra wastes. Red deer, wild oxen and wild pig now provided the basic needs of thinly spread hunter communities from places like King Arthur's Cave.

The Boreal phase, starting about 7500 bc, brought in hazel, pine and oak forest; and possibly saw intrusive Mesolithic groups competing for game and maybe herding deer and oxen. A barbed antler point from an ancient pond at Llanybodwel, south of Oswestry will belong to this phase. However most Mesolithic immigration to the Marches was probably delayed until the Atlantic phase, 5500 bc, when a moister, maritime climate resulted in a higher forest of oak and elm.

Microliths are few in the Marches, even along the Clun-Clee Ridgeway zone where field-workers have long been active. They come from hilltop locations in south-east Shropshire (fig 5, 11-16) and on Chase Hill, Ross; and from valleys at Arrow Court and Lower Harpton near Kington. Some have recently been found in the Forest of Dean.

Hunting or herding parties may be expected to choose well-drained camp sites close to springs or streams and most of the sites noted above conform to such requirements, but unlike Mesolithic camp sites in south-east and north-east England, most finds in the Marches are loosely associated with larger quantities of later material. Thus Chase Hill offers one microlith among a quantity of Neolithic scrapers and Gamage Farm, Much Marcle, a handful of Mesolithic flints with many Neolithic tools. More finds have been coming from valley gravels and more might be anticipated along the shores of pro-glacial lakes around Wigmore, Church Stretton and the middle Severn. These would have been good places to obtain wildfowl as well as venison and wild pig.

The descendants of these hunters, whose remains are so elusive, may have become the guides, porters and perhaps stockmen for subsequent Neolithic people. To that extent the sparse Mesolithic occupation may have paved the way for the penetration of Neolithic ideas and trade.

CHAPTER THREE

Neolithic settlers and Traders

The Neolithic in Britain began around 3500 bc, equivalent to 4200 BC on the dendrochronological calendar. This long formative period contin- ued until Beaker pottery heralded the advent of metallurgy about 2000 bc (2520 BC). The line between Neolithic and Beaker periods in the border can only be tentative but there are sufficient indications of the new religious, social and economic developments to justify the notion of a definite Beaker phase. So most Beaker period finds are here put in Chapter 4.

We know much about Neolithic tombs but little about settle- ments. We do not know whether those buried in chamber tombs were local people or whether the few clusters of tombs received the dead from miles around. The economy of contemporary communities in Europe was based on agriculture; but in the early years game from the forest may have supplemented the diet. Some Mesolithic hunters will have survived but so far we have no dated cultural assemblages as proof of this.

Let us return to Sudbrook which in Neolithic times would have been a kilometre or more inland, the coast approximating to the present five-fathom contour. A Neolithic skull and animal bones were found six metres below sea-level at Newport; and a polished Neolithic axe is among finds from the Severn Levels. Submerged forests and a mesolithic footprint in silt have been dated off-shore there recently.

Numerous chamber tombs, the Severn-Cotswold Group, are distributed across the water in Somerset and to the west in South Wales and the Black Mountains. Some have transepted stone chambers reached by a narrow passage from the broad end of a covering long mound; others have lateral chambers entered from the side of the mound. The transepted form has parallels in north-west France, whence too the idea of lateral chambers may have come. We can imagine both types being introduced by settlers and missionaries arriving by sea to land near Sudbrook at the head of the estuary. The final form of most tombs could have emerged from local development, for they have a long history as shown by dates of 3885 BC for a Neolithic pit under Gwernvale tomb and 3805 BC for bones from Pen y Wyrlod, both in Powys. These two are part of a group of at least seventeen tombs around the Black Mountains that fall mostly outside our special field of study. Savory has argued that the area may have been reached from Dyfed by way of the upper Usk Valley. On the other hand, the presence of both terminally and laterally chambered tombs on both sides of the

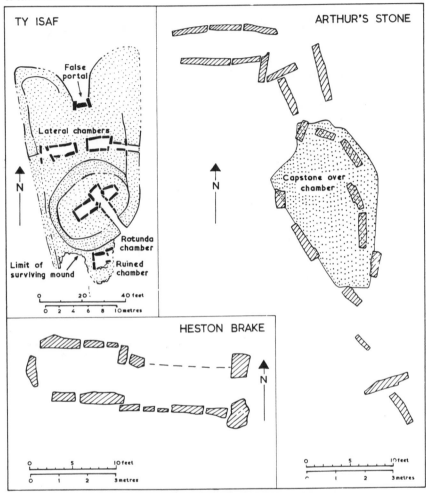

Fig 7 Chamber tomb plans: the remaining orthostats of Arthur's Stone
(after RCHM England 1932) and Heston Brake (after Daniel
1950) with Ty Isaf, Powys for comparison (after Grimes 1939)

Severn estuary may show the parallel development, if not unity, of the
two parts of the Severn-Cotswold region. The Heston Brake tomb, on
a low hill just inland from Sudbrook, is sited as though commemorat-
ing a landing. Upright stones, or orthostats, define a terminal chamber
and passage (fig 7). Little of the former mound remains. An excavation
in 1888 uncovered skeletons and some post-Neolithic artefacts.

   North-west of Heston Brake a ridge leads to hills that extend
from Chepstow Park to Wentwood. Along that ridge, beside the road,

Plate 7   Arthur's Stone chamber tomb, Dorstone from north-west.
            See fig 7

are the remains of another megalithic chamber tomb, Y Gaer Llwyd, Newchurch West. Five orthostats and a capstone, along with some recumbent stones, mark this second monument to the piety of our Neolithic pioneers, 213 metres above sea-level in a col at the head of valleys on either side of the ridge. It is well placed as a first stage on the path to the Black Mountains but it stands alone. There is no other tomb until those by Crickhowell are reached, forty-two kilometres from Heston Brake and not much more from Swansea Bay.

Other evidence of Neolithic occupation in Gwent includes a flint axe from Gwernesney, Usk and a polished stone axe from Chepstow. Five more sites have produced stone tools appropriate to the late Neolithic or Beaker period, including a flint sickle from Usk.

Of the Black Mountain sites, our area includes the ruined tomb of Arthur's Stone and the long barrow presumed to cover such a tomb at Cross Lodge Farm, both in Dorstone parish. The former is at 268 metres on the ridge between the Wye and Dore whereas Cross Lodge barrow is on the lower slope, two kilometres away, at 167 metres.

Arthur's Stone (fig 7 ; pl 7) has an irregular polygonal main chamber about 5 .5 metres long covered by an enormous capstone of a local limestone concretion, cornstone, and parts of at least two passages or chambers at the north end. A wide orthostat with cup-marks, standing across the major axis south-east of the main chamber, looks like a false portal, as would be appropriate in a laterally chambered Severn-Cotswold tomb. The covering mound, pillaged years ago, once showed to the south and must have extended north as well.

In the same area literary accounts imply a chamber tomb in Park Wood, St Margarets. Others may await recognition but northwards the only accepted record of a chamber tomb, now destroyed, is of Llech y Wydhon on Llanymynech Hill. Three alleged chamber tombs in the Shropshire parishes of Norton-in-Hales and Highley, and on Stapeley Hill, the Giant's Grave or Cave, were rejected by Daniel.

The Herefordshire tombs thus stand at the edge of a Neolithic burial area. Nearby, on the slopes of Cefn Hill at over 450 metres, Gavin-Robinson found leaf-shaped arrowheads, spindle-whorls and many flakes of flint beneath the peat. There was also a small sandstone mortar and a pebble hammerstone thought to have been used to crack the numerous hazelnut shells found there. Many flint sites have been mapped along the ridge; and many leaf-shaped arrowheads and pieces of polished stone axe have been recorded at Vowchurch and on the Merbach ridge at Stockley Hill, Woodbury Hill and Arthur's Stone.

Away from the Black Mountains, the few sites yielding numerous flakes and arrowheads include Fownhope, Wellington Heath, Keephill and Hanley William, all on hills under 180 metres above sea-level. The presence of barbed and tanged arrowheads of the Beaker period along with leaf-shaped ones and fragments of polished flint axes (fig 8) on sites like Keephill shows they were used more than once. They may have been permanent dwelling sites.

Our attention has so far been directed to sites on hilltops and ridgeways but many Neolithic finds come from middle slopes and even valley floors, notably those of the Arrow above Kington and around Titley and Staunton, and of the Teme at Bucknell and Buckton. This ubiquity of Neolithic finds extends also to axes. From Herefordshire there are at least fifteen complete stone and six complete flint axes in a total of thirty-six axe finds: too many too widely scattered to be losses by transitory traders. They derive from most of the main British polished stone axe areas. The Group I greenstone axes from Elton and St Margarets must have come from the neighbourhood of Penzance; a

Fig 8 Herefordshire Neolithic and Beaker tools. X½ except 10 (¼).

1 & 2 Leaf-shaped arrowheads	8 Polished stone axe
3 Petit-tranchet derivative arrowhead	9 Polished flint axe
4 Barbed and tanged arrowhead	10 Perforated axe hammer
5 Plano-convex knife	11 Battle axe
6 & 7 Scrapers	10 & 11 are both of Corndon picrite

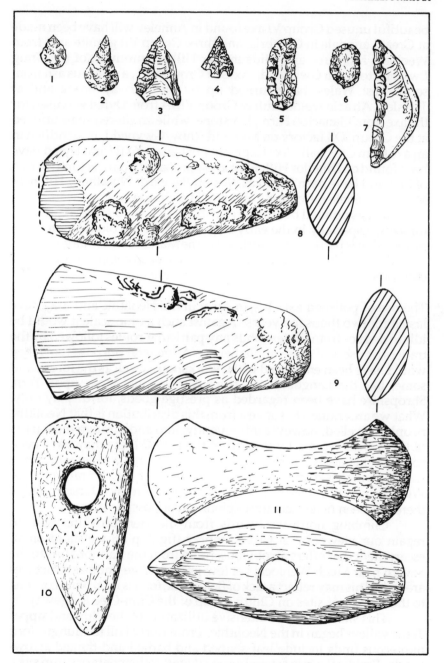

beautiful unused Group VI axe found in Almeley will have been made at Great Langdale in Cumbria; and three Group VII granite axes from Weobley, Mocktree and Midsummer Hill are products of the Graig Lwyd factories in Gwynedd. Axes of Group VIII, a siliceous ash from south-west Wales, have turned up by the Garway Brook and at Tupsley. An acid welded tuff of Group VIIIA from Dyfed was used for the axe from Llanarfon Farm, Dorstone; while an altered shale utilized at the Group XXI factory on Mynydd Rhiw, Gwynedd, is identified in an axe from Craswall. Axe fragments of Group XXII from Dyfed have been found on Dinedor Hill. Flint axes, probably from the south or east of England have been found at Weston Beggard, Woodbury Hill near Moccas, Weobley, Dorstone Hill and Hunderton.

Briggs pointed out that erratic boulders could serve as quarries for axes, especially in the early stage of Neolithic colonization. The proposition is particularly pertinent in the Marches where large erratics from the Lake District and Wales must have been common. Such local enterprise need not rule out the use of distant outcrops.

The use of polished axes began early in the Neolithic and may have lasted for two thousand years. Against such a time-scale it would be idle to deduce from the few finds any particular routes followed by the traders or users of these implements. As general purpose tools they would have been employed in the workshop as well as the forest; and some, like the Langdale axes from Almeley and Stoke-upon-Tern, Shropshire have been regarded as prestige goods, for display only. What we are entitled to suggest from this distribution is that Neolithic people travelled, however infrequently, into and through most parts of this varied region. By the end of the period there may have been considerable areas cleared for grazing, and even arable, with some sizeable villages dispersed across the width of the central Marches. With the exception of some trial excavations on the Dorstone ridge there has been no systematic exploration of possible sites.

Climbing north-westwards from the Herefordshire plain to regain our viewpoint at Croft Ambrey (fig 3, p 5) we stand on an escarpment that offers an obvious route from the Radnor Hills to the Severn near Much Wenlock; yet few pre-Iron Age finds or structures are on it. This may reflect a lack of fieldwork, for it is in striking contrast to the density of sites on Chitty's map of the Clun-Clee Ridgeway.

This shows that the intensive utilization of the Clun and upper Teme valleys began in the Neolithic. From Kerry Hill to Clungunford numerous finds include leaf-shaped and barbed-and-tanged arrowheads. Prolific flints in several areas suggest settlements or camp sites.

As Chitty observed, the finds are not restricted to the Ridgeway but occur broadly to north and south with a moderate density extending six or seven kilometres from the ridge. Some concentrations are only a kilometre from one another and are found at all levels, from the flood plains to the tops of the interfluves - from 150 to 400 metres. Around Clunbury there is a find-spot for every 3.5 square kilometres. No Neolithic polished axes have been found on the Ridgeway; those from Oakly Park and Kinlet were about a kilometre from the route.

Neolithic potsherds have been found on later hillforts at the Roveries near Bishop's Castle and, in Powys, at Fridd Faldwyn and the Breidden. In this context, Arnold has pointed to the possibility of the first phase of the Fridd Faldwyn defences being Neolithic in date, as at Crickley Hill near Cheltenham. It raises questions about the earliest phases of some of the hillforts in between. At lower levels, some kind of settlement is indicated by Neolithic pottery and hazel-nut shells from two small pits at Bromfield dated about 3,500 BC.

It is time to move northwards once again to the Wrekin where, in 1973, a barbed and tanged arrowhead was found. In the Shropshire lowlands before us (fig 4, p 9) Neolithic finds include a handful of polished axes: two from near Oswestry were possibly from Mynydd Rhiw; another at Stoke-upon-Tern from Langdale; and there are flint examples from Shakeford, Hinstock, Hadnall and Uppington. Another axe from Hinstock may have come from Penzance and a Group XX axe from Harley (fig 3, p 5) is probably from Charnwood Forest, Leicestershire. Group XV rock, probably from the Lake District, was used for the cylindrical axe from Attingham Park. Sherds of Neolithic bowls have been found on a lowland site by Sharpstone Hill near Shrewsbury.

Chitty often underlined the importance of the Severn valley gravels for settlement and trade; and most of these locations are close to the river. This riverside pattern extends south to Leighton and into the central Marches with a Great Langdale axe at Alveley (fig 3, p 5). Not that the river had a monopoly of trade; numerous axes in the hills suggest that tracks criss-crossed this territory.

In Cheshire the distribution of polished stone axes is widespread. They come from coastal sites in the Wirral and both valley and hill locations inland; more than thirty from Cheshire as a whole. Beyond the plain of the Dee and west of Moel y Gaer the ascent of the Clwyds takes us out of our region of study and into territory with more evidence of occupation; at the northern end of these hills, overlooking Prestatyn, sites like the Gop Cave and King Charles Bowling Green, Gwaenysgor, have yielded quantities of Neolithic material.

CHAPTER FOUR

The border in Beaker times

Around 2500 BC the working of copper and gold was brought to Ireland by adventurous artisans who probably came from Beaker groups in Atlantic Europe. While they were persuading their Neolithic hosts that a cast copper axe was cheaper or more efficient than the old stone implements the influence of Beaker cultures in the south and east of Britain led to the development of a large market for the new tools. The raw material was restricted to the west - exploited first in Ireland but later in Cornwall, Wales and the Lake District. The stone axe trade had already shown the way to carry western goods to south-eastern markets.

The Marches were probably only lightly populated in Neolithic times and the rarity of known beakers and copper tools makes it unlikely that there was a sudden change in population now. Beaker sherds have been found as secondary deposits in the south Powys chamber tombs and the barbed and tanged flint arrowheads that accompany Beakers have come from open sites on the Black Mountains and elsewhere. Many of these have also yielded Neolithic leaf-shaped arrowheads. Changes in burial custom are illustrated by two stone-lined cists discovered on the side of the Olchon valley, each containing a skeleton and a beaker (pl 8). In a cairn over 600 metres above sea-level near the summit of Pen Gloch y Pibwr, north of Crickhowell, a handled beaker was found. In east Herefordshire a beaker is recorded at Mathon and beaker sherds were found in Midsummer Hill Camp.

At Aymestrey gravel quarry, a stone cist was uncovered with a beaker and skeleton inside. The gravel site at Bromfield had beaker sherds in an apparently domestic context beneath a barrow dated around 1800 cal BC. Parts of two stone slabs on the edge of the barrow might have been the remains of a cist burial. On nearby Sheet Hill, Ludlow, beaker sherds were found; and the lowland site of Sharpstone Hill, Shrewsbury, had beaker sherds as well as an enlarged food vessel containing a cremation. At Four Crosses. Llandysilio, in Powys, a Beaker inhumation grave with a V-perforated jet or shale button, was inserted in a Neolithic oval barrow; from a shallow pit, centring on 2275 cal BC, came Beaker sherds and grains of barley. At Trelystan, also just in Powys on the eastern slope of the Long Mountain, Beaker sherds are thought to represent domestic activity following a late Neolithic occupation of stake-walled huts. Such continuity from Neolithic to

Plate 9 A reconstructed beaker from the Olchon
valley cist burials, 190 mm high
(Hereford City Museums)

Beaker occupation suggests that some important Neolithic locations
remained the foci of activity with old routes still in use.

It is appropriate that we now view the Clun-Clee Ridgeway (fig
3) which Chitty saw becoming important with the trade in perforated
battle-axes and axe-hammers, type fossils of the Beaker cultures. It lies
for the most part on the ridge between the Clun and Teme. From Kerry
Hill by way of the destroyed Grey Stones circle, Bettws-Y-Crwyn
church, Spoad Hill and the Llwyn, it arrives at Rock Hill and then Cwm
on Black Hill before descending to cross the Clun at Clungunford. It
is then held to go over May Hill and Brand Hill where one prolific flint
site and a handful of other find-spots lie reasonably close, and then
descend to cross the Onny at Onnibury. The suggested course goes
through the Bromfield barrow area and across the Corve near Ludlow.
It then follows the modern road on to the west slopes of Titterstone Clee
and goes on towards Farlow and Prescott. Veering south-east it then
drops to Bewdley and the Severn. East of May Hill the only clusters of
finds are at Bromfield, Farlow, Oreton and Prescott.

Five perforated battle-axes and axe-hammers have been found within a kilometre of the route: at Hopton Castle, Bromfield, Bitterley, east of Titterstone Clee and Farlow. The few datable associations of such implements are of the Copper or Early Bronze Age and they have a general association with Beakers. They were made from a variety of igneous rocks and were disseminated widely in southern Britain. One large group, XII, is of picrite from Corndon Hill just over the Powys boundary. Their distribution to the Midlands might have involved the Ridgeway but they are widespread in the Marches. Nearly seventy per cent of those originally identified were found within thirty-two kilometres of the source, implying that the majority were for home consumption. They point to increased local activity as well as to trade between the quarries and communities as far away as Cambridgeshire. Several similar implements of foreign rock may point to gift exchange with distant communities: the Kington axe-hammer, for example, was made of Group XXIIIb quartz-dolerite from Dyfed.

Four picrite axes between Shrewsbury and Montford Bridge may show routes to and from Corndon focusing on fordable stretches of the Severn. Two implements of another rock were found by the river at Wroxeter; at Brompton Ford nearby, a large broken axe-hammer was of Group XV rock. In Shropshire north of the Severn there are at least nine such tools of various rocks; and in Cheshire many occur along the central ridge as well as in the Wirral and elsewhere.

Stone circles too may span the Copper and Early Bronze Age. Seldom datable, they are regarded as later than chamber tombs because of their geographical separateness and greater altitudinal range. Two lie north of Corndon Hill: Mitchell's Fold (fig 9) and the Hoarstones.

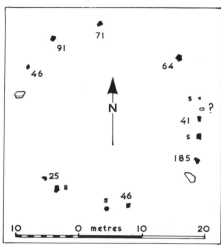

Fig 9 Mitchell's Fold stone circle, after Grimes 1963. Height of standing stones in cms; stone stumps marked 's'; and recumbent stones blank.

The former is the better exposed, about 366 metres above sea-level with a wide and exciting view west over Wales. Here on the roof of their world the local prehistoric inhabitants erected a circle 26-27.4 metres diameter in which fourteen or fifteen stones survive in place, most less than a metre high and the highest nearly two metres. Two and a half kilometres north-east, in a swampy hollow just east of the ridge, is the Hoarstones circle, 23-24 metres across, originally having thirty-eight stones, most of them now buried in peat.

Stone circles presumably had some ritual or astronomical purpose and are not all that common. Grimes' map of those in Wales and the border shows that they tend to occur in small groups as though their congregations were restricted to small areas, or more likely that a few important centres served wide areas. Mitchell's Fold and the Hoarstones mark the Corndon-Shelve area as one of these; its main catchment may be indicated by the distribution of the picrite axes, extending about thirty-two kilometres from the hill.

A related type of monument, the embanked earth circle, combining a setting of stones with an earth ring-work, was also possibly present in south Shropshire on the Clun-Clee Ridgeway. The destroyed Grey Stones, near the boundary with Wales, formerly had a ring-wall about thirty metres diameter overall with kerbs of large blocks. Another circle on the same route at Pen y Wern, Clun may be the remains of a denuded cairn twenty-seven metres diameter. The Bicton burial circle near Clun may also belong to this period, carrying a mutilated Neolithic stone axe of Charnwood Forest rock on the cairn above a cremation burial. Near the summit of Titterstone Clee, O'Neil excavated a walled 'Earth Circle' a metre high and eighteen metres across that covered a pit three metres deep. Bicton is by the Clun; the rest are high: Pen-y-Wern 381 metres, the Grey Stones 441 metres and Titterstone Clee 533 metres.

Garn-Wen in the Black Mountains is another possible site, at 472 metres. There is a doubtful record of three stones, the Whetstones, south of Mitchell's Fold: and there are eleven stones of what might once have been an ancient circle at Penbedw Park, Cilcain on the Clwyd-Dee watershed. In most parts of the Marches posts probably provided equivalents for stones; unless surrounded by a ditch they are unlikely to be found.

Standing stones may also be a part of the Beaker contribution to the landscape. On the north-west edge of the Forest of Dean are two single stones. In Marion's Enclosure, Staunton, on the north side of the road, the stone is at 206 metres. By contrast, the Queen Stone at Huntsham stands beside the river Wye. It is local sandstone 4.5 metres long with 2.4 metres below the modern ground level. Sharply cut

Plate 9 Harold's Stones, Trelleck from the south

grooves up to 170 millimetres deep run vertically to ground level but not below, five on the south-east face, three opposite, and two and one on the others. Some may have originated from weathering since the stone was erected but their depth and sharp form suggests human improvement, not necessarily in ancient times. In east Gwent by Trelleck, on the limestone plateau 213 metres above sea-level, three large ones, Harold's Stones, are set in line. Cup-marks on them include two on the centre one about 180 millimetres diameter (pl 9). The modern village, once a borough, is a centre for the surrounding area. This spot was a focus in prehistoric times too.

CHAPTER FIVE

Bronze Age Developments

By 2000 BC bronze was replacing copper for cutting tools and weapons. Many of the items shown on fig 10 may have been brought into the Marches by traders but others will have been made locally. The early metal axes were flat but in the Middle Bronze Age the palstave was developed with provision for seating the haft. Chitty long ago saw that the metallurgical similarity of the flat axe and unlooped palstave from Asterton Prolley Moor pointed to the use of local ores; and the discovery of the multiple flat axe mould at Longden Common, close to copper-bearing pre-Cambrian rocks near Pontesbury, adds to the case for a Shropshire industry in the Early Bronze Age.

Rowlands has shown the development of regional traditions in much of southern England in the Middle Bronze Age but it is not yet clear whether the Marches had its own distinct traditions. The uncertainty continues into the Late Bronze Age, after 1000 BC, when the similarity of border weapons with others far away led Burgess to propound a single cultural and political region stretching from the Wash to Cardigan Bay, dominated by warriors armed with spears of the type best known from Broadward, Shropshire. It is likely, however, to be misleading to use any single artefactual criterion such as bronzework to distinguish cultures and thereby imply political regions.

The distribution of barrows has sometimes been seen to reflect agricultural exploitation. This has led to the idea that barrows on hills since covered by peat show that an uphill movement during a drier period in the Early Bronze Age was followed by a retreat downhill during the Late Bronze Age. In this area however there is no dating for most barrows and a general ignorance of settlements. The barrows and other cemeteries might be located for special religious or topographical reasons, related only distantly to the homes of those buried in them. In the Marches there are already sufficient dated burials to show that the hilltops never had a monopoly in funerals.

A convenient summary of Bronze Age finds, but including Beaker material, was provided by Chitty and Fox, as map C in Personality of Britain and the relative regional densities remain valid, though new studies and distribution maps have been made by Burgess and Cowan, by Rowlands, by Burgess, Coombs and Davies, and by Freke and Holgate. There is a scatter of finds along the uplands of the southern border with a concentration in the Black Mountains; and a cluster

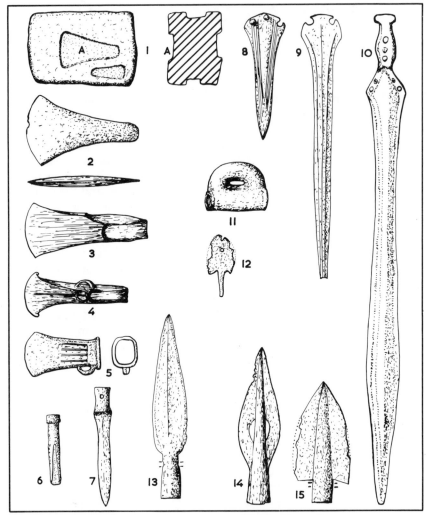

Fig 10 Bronze Age implements from the Welsh Marches. All x 1/5
except Nos 1 (4/25) and 11 (2/5). All bronze except 1.

1 Multiple flat-axe mould of stone
  from Longden Common: one face
  and cross-section
2 Flat axe, Newcastle-on-Clun
3 Flanged axe, Bucknell
4 Looped palstave, Ross
5 Socketed axe, St Arvans
6 Socketed gouge, Brogyntyn
7 Socketed knife, Minera

8 Ogival dagger, Ebnal
9 Rapier, Aston Ingham
10 Leaf-shaped sword, Cwm-du
11 D-shaped tube, purpose
  uncertain, Broadward
12 Tanged razor, Merlin's Cave
13 Socketed spearhead, Guilsfield
14 Socketed spearhead, Willowmoor
15 Barbed spearhead, Broadward

lines the Severn from Bridgnorth to Worcester. By contrast, the Hereford plain and the uplands to the west are almost empty. Finds recur in some number across the hills of the central Marches from the Severn to the upper Teme. To the north again the western sides of the Cheshire and Shropshire plains show an overflow from the dense patches recorded over North Wales. Apart from these foothill finds the main occurrence of Bronze Age material in the northern Marches is along the sandstone ridge from the Mersey near Helsby to the hills between Wem and Hodnet. Most of these finds are perforated Beaker implements; Bronze Age evidence is more scattered. The ridge offers a trade link between the Mersey and middle Severn but many of the finds could derive from east or west of the ridge and may have been supplied to settlers on the ridge itself.

The Dean-Trelleck uplands (fig 2, fig 10)

In the Early and Middle Bronze Age the coastal zone appears to have been more important than the uplands. Savory saw the coastal barrows as evidence of settlement from Somerset whereas Grimes thought they were more likely to show the adoption of a new burial fashion by local Neolithic people. He drew upon the evidence from the Crick House, Caerwent bell-barrow where a leaf-shaped arrowhead and two plano-convex flint knives were found. Like the cup-marked stones around the barrow, such tools are regarded as Neolithic.

The excavation of St Bride's Netherwent barrow in 1860 produced fragments of a bronze dagger blade, and there is another barrow mound at Langstone, thirty metres diameter. Two collared urns come from Usk and a bronze flat axe from nearby. Middle Bronze Age palstaves come from Liswerry, Caldicot, Goytre, Newport and Llantilio Crossenny.

An Early Bronze Age axe comes from Monmouth; but most of the finds from the uplands between the Usk and the Wye belong to the Late Bronze Age. By the park gate of Llantilio Court a fragmentary leaf-shaped arrowhead was found and socketed axes come from near Trelleck, Castle Hill Usk, Gwehelog, Llanarth and Llanfair Court. Founders' hoards containing outmoded implements and scrap for reworking are particularly common in the Late Bronze Age: the one from Llanddewi Rhydderch included two looped socketed axes. Two more such axes, of Breton type, were found on Chapel Hill, Tintern; and a hoard of seven were found near Liveoaks Farm, St Arvans.

Even allowing for the greater abundance of bronze generally in the Late Bronze Age the increased number of find sites seems to betoken an intensified colonization. A post-ring house has recently been excavated at Chapel Tump and Late Bronze Age occupation identified at Cold Harbour. Despite the rarity of such undefended homesteads in the archaeological record, it is tempting to assume an increase in population and to associate this with the first appearance of hillforts. Savory has pointed to the possibility of a Late Bronze Age date for the promontory sites of the Wye valley, drawing our attention particularly to the finds from Merlin's Cave near Symonds Yat promontory fort. They included a disc-headed and a rolled-strip headed pin of a type associated with continental, hillfort-building, Urnfield cultures. A slotted spool from the same cave is similar to the form from Dinorben hillfort, Clwyd and there was also a maple-leaf bronze razor. The leaf-shaped sword from Garn Wen, Cwm-du at 427 metres in the Black Mountains attests a continuing interest in high places in the Late Bronze Age.

The agricultural potential of the Herefordshire basin was not to be realized during the Bronze Age and most artefacts and barrows are around the sides. Lacking settlements we can only consider the stray finds and barrow distribution, few of them without problems of authentication. Thus there is doubt about the bronzes, including palstaves and spearheads, from Netherwood and Kyre Park. They are possibly from a hoard thought to have been deposited in a quarry near the former St Michael's College, Tenbury Wells after being stolen from one of the masters' collection.

Round barrows, though most common in the Bronze Age, may cover burials of any period from Neolithic to Saxon; and they may be confused with windmill mounds, as at Shobdon, or with mottes. The latter can often be distinguished by the presence of an attached bailey; and where the mound lies next to a medieval church it is most likely to be a motte as is the case at St Weonards. With these cautions, it is likely that there are about twenty-six Bronze Age barrows recognized in Herefordshire and four more that appear as ring-ditches on aerial photographs. Two cemeteries are known: one at Southend Farm, Mathon and the other at Pontshill, south-east of Ross.

The Mathon cemetery showed during sand quarrying from 1910 onwards and the record of the finds is casual indeed. Fragments of two looped spearheads were found in black deposits suggestive of cremated burials and many urns with cremated bones were found, some buried in lines. The few urns that survive include a fine collared one in Hereford Museum and parts of others resembling some of the Bromfield material. There was also a beaker and some Iron Age and Roman sherds. A nearby ring-ditch was photographed by Baker. These finds are sufficient to indicate the possibility of other intensively utilized locations appearing elsewhere in the Herefordshire lowlands.

On the nearby Malvern ridge at Colwall there are two barrows; and from Midsummer Hill have come some probable Bronze Age sherds and a palstave.

The view from here north-westwards would have been mostly across virgin forest, all the way to the Radnor and Wigmore hills. Just here and there would have been clearings, like the one near Wellington where the author photographed a couple of ring-ditches. In contrast, the land between Midsummer Hill and the Black Mountains has ample evidence for this period. There is a possible barrow, Bagpiper's Tump, in the Woolhope Hills near Mordiford, and a looped palstave was found on Oldbury Camp. Further south, finds around Ross include a flanged axe, rapier and spearhead from Aston Ingham, a palstave from Weston-under-Penyard, another spearhead from Coughton Marsh and a further palstave (fig 10) from somewhere near Ross. At Pontshill, a finger-decorated urn was found 450 millimetres below the surface resting on a layer of charcoal - apparently a cremation burial.

In south-west Herefordshire, near Tram Inn, was found an unlooped palstave with ribbed shield ornament. Two palstaves and a socketed axe come from Vowchurch and another socketed axe from Llanthony Abbey. There are two barrows on the plain at Madley, two at Michaelchurch and others at Tyberton, Turnastone, Abbey Dore, Craswall and Dorstone.

These signs of Bronze Age activity across south Herefordshire may relate to the sandier soils in contrast to the clays that cover most of north Herefordshire. The only bronze artefacts found distant from the hills in that county are a bronze ferrule from St Margaret's Park, Hereford, a leaf-shaped sword and spatulate dagger from Fayre Oaks, Hereford and a socketed knife from Lyonshall. The dagger is Middle Bronze Age but the rest are late forms and consistent with a Late Bronze Age initiative in the exploitation of the lowlands.

The central Marches (fig 3, p 5)

No Bronze Age artefacts were found at Croft Ambrey hillfort although, inexplicably, a date of 1000 cal BC was obtained for some carbonized grain. A potsherd, formerly open to be Bronze Age, is now matched by Iron Age sherds with the same dolerite temper at Bromfield. Near Croft Castle a ring-ditch, photographed from the air, may be a barrow; and within Brandon Camp a barrow ditch was partly excavated. Otherwise, in this hilly district, most barrows presently known are on valley floors. Three are recorded by the Lugg around Kinsham; another near Walford is probably the survivor of three there.

The incidence of valleyward barrows is high enough to show

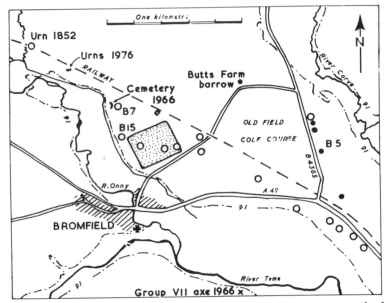

Fig 11 The Bromfield necropolis. Five upstanding barrows are marked by large dots; the fourteen ploughed-down or quarried ones by circles. The Roman marching camp and Iron Age farm north of it are stippled.

that rivers held a special place in the minds of the Bronze Age people. It could be that they farmed the lighter soils on river terraces and buried their dead no distance from their farms; but equally the deceased may have been brought down to the river from afar. We may note that the round barrow at Jacket's Well, Knighton, which produced two collared urns and cremated bones, was at a confluence. In the area of the Clun-Teme confluence by Leintwardine there are at least eight ring-ditches on aerial photographs in addition to the Walford barrows.

The Bromfield necropolis

Between the limestone hills above Leintwardine and the dominating brow of Titterstone Clee is the confluence of the Corve, Onny and Teme, framing a gravel terrace that extends from Bromfield to Ludlow. An oval area 1500 metres long and 750 metres wide was occupied by some twenty barrows and at least three prehistoric flat cemeteries. Two big barrows border the golf course and a huge one, much reduced by ploughing, is in the angle between the railway and the B4365.

In 1884 Fortey found cremated bones and part of a bronze knife at the bottom of the Butts Farm barrow. In digging the other tree-crowned mound B5 a large urn near the top was broken. This and the heavily decorated enlarged food vessel from the barrow cut by the railway in 1852 should date around 1600 BC; but the area had been in use much earlier. A Neolithic axe, a battle axe and Neolithic and Beaker sherds have been found here.

A carbon-14 date of 2560 BC was obtained for charcoal in a pit cut by the ditch of barrow B7 excavated in advance of quarrying in 1967. The central grave was empty but around the barrow and up to twenty metres from it were several grave deposits including four urns; three were upright, one on its side. There were also four small deposits of washed cremated bone and two shallow pits containing charcoal.

In 1981 a layer of pyre charcoal was found under the remains of a barrow, B15, which covered two unurned cremations. The three dates of the pyre and cremations lie between 1945 and 1725 cal BC. Beaker sherds were found beneath, and possible remains of a Beaker cist on the edge of the barrow. If this was a secondary Beaker burial the barrow itself should be Beaker. The dates are appropriate. One of the pits of a small adjacent cemetery was dated 1400 cal BC.

Thirty metres west of barrow B7 was cemetery C1 with some 130 shallow pits up to 600 millimetres diameter. The new Stuiver/Pearson calibration dates the earliest of its dated graves to 1270 cal BC and the latest to 870 cal BC; a third grave was dated 955 cal BC. This halves the original estimate of the cemetery's use, bringing it down to about 400 years. Continuity of use during this time is shown by the rarity of instances where one grave cuts another. The earth mound that was surplus to filling requirements was adequately prominent to ensure that its position was respected, even over centuries.

Only two graves had cremated bones in urns. These had first been placed in holes 600 millimetres deep. A token of the cremation was then poured in and the grave backfilled. There were instances where only a compact deposit of cremated bone was encountered, as though it had been held in a cloth or leather bag; and there were twenty-two pits with nothing but charcoal below their backfilling. The other hundred pits contained various amounts of comminuted cremated bone in a charcoal deposit, and of these thirty-one had some pottery. In many cases most of the pot had been buried, but only after being smashed. There was no evidence of more than one vessel in any pit.

The pottery displays several of the ornamental features - such as imitation horseshoe handles, bosses and finger-tip decoration - found on urns of the Deverel-Rimbury tradition of southern Britain (fig 12). Although the styles originated elsewhere, the pots themselves were

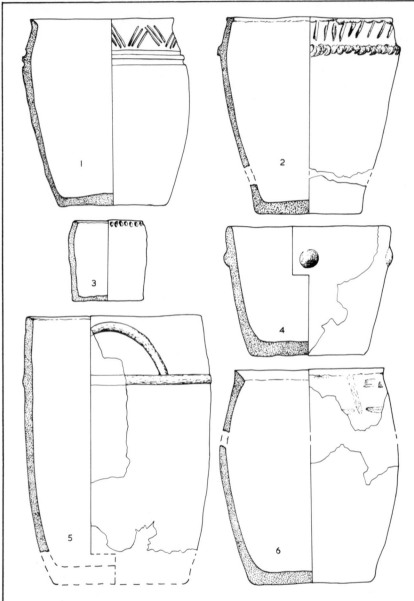

Fig 12   Some of the pottery from Bromfield cemetery C1 (1/4), Nos 1,2
and 6 from pits dated 1270 cal BC, 955 cal BC and 870 cal BC
respectively. Note the finger-tipping on No. 3, the bosses on
No. 4 and the applied horseshoe decoration on No. 5.

made nearby using Clee Hill dolerite for tempering. We may speculate whether they were provided for the lowlanders by a Clee Hill firm of professional potters or funeral directors, or whether the cemetery was reserved for people from the Clee Hills, twelve kilometres to the east. The first is probably the case but the concentration of barrows and focal position of the necropolis makes likely its use by neighbouring communities. The idea might be tested if the quarry uncovers further cemeteries where different tempering is found in the pottery.

There are few other Bronze Age burial sites in this sector of the Marches. A barrow containing three skeletons in separate stone cists was removed when Ludlow church was built. On Titterstone Clee is a cairn close to the crag known as the Giant's Chair, and there is another barrow at Coreley. A seated skeleton was found in a mound when the new church was built at Farlow; and at Dowles near Bewdley there is an old record of a probable cemetery and aerial photographs of ring-ditches on the terrace gravels there.

In south-west Shropshire and Powys barrows occur both on the hills and on the valley floors. One is mapped beside the river at Eaton in Lydbury North parish and another between the Unk and Clun south of Bicton where two more have shown as circular crop marks caused by improved growth over the deeper soil in their ditches. Barrows are found in the hills east of Church Stoke and several more along the Shropshire/Powys border; but the greatest concentration is on the Long Mynd where twenty occur at around 427 metres. They are often placed near the edge, on view from the neighbouring valley. In view of its height and steep slopes it is difficult to regard the Long Mynd as a favoured farming region; more likely they brought their dead, if only their most respected leaders, this high to lie close to the clouds.

These barrows probably, however, indicate that the surrounding area was well populated. Certainly, as Chitty demonstrated, the products of many workshops came this way, presumably in part for local use. Early in the metal age decorated flat axes of Irish type were lost on Titterstone Clee and in Clunbury, and other flat axes at Arley on the Severn, at Newcastle-on-Clun and at Castle Bryn Amlwg.

The more developed form of axe, the palstave, was essentially a tool of the Middle Bronze Age but survived after 900 BC into the Late Bronze Age. Four have been found around Bewdley and another at Eardington near Bridgnorth. Another group appears by Leintwardine with provenanced finds at Walford and Buckton; and a flanged axe comes from Bucknell. Other palstaves are listed from Upper Woodhouse Farm, Knighton, from Bryn Shop, Castle Bryn Amlwg and from Titterstone Clee. A socketed axe was found at Upper House Farm, Silvington.

Two Late Bronze Age metal hoards have been found during draining operations in the central Marches. The small one from the Bloody Romans field, Lydham Heath included spearheads, one of them lunate, and parts of three swords, one being leaf-shaped. The other hoard was found at Broadward Hall, Clungunford in 1867, nearly two metres down, with many animal bones including complete skulls. The surviving items, now in the British Museum, include parts of at least forty-six spearheads, twenty being barbed. There were also seven pieces of spearhead sockets, five ferrules, two bugle-shaped objects, a tanged chisel and eleven leaf-shaped sword fragments. As with the earlier confluence barrows, the location of these hoards probably reflects a special interest in water for ritual acts with weapons being sacrificed to propitiate the gods. Burgess has suggested that the Broadward metalwork tradition, stretching from Lincolnshire to Dyfed, was established in a society in which a water cult thrived.

During this period forest clearance was probably intensified to feed an increased population, coinciding roughly with a climatic change about 800 BC from the drier sub-Boreal continental climate to the wet and cloudy Atlantic phase. Together with deforestation this resulted in greatly increased run-off, repeatedly flooding the valleys and burying their plains in silt. Among the losses may have been the workplaces and stock-in-trade of riverside bronze-smiths. The fortunate ones will have escaped the flood in dug-out canoes like the two from Marton Pool, Chirbury which probably belong to this period.

The Shrewsbury plain and the Dee and Weaver valleys (fig 4)

North of the Severn, Bronze Age material earlier than about 1400 BC is infrequent. What there is lies across the south-western part from Hadley near the Wrekin to Oswestry and the valley of the Ceiriog beyond. The flat axes of Hadley and Battlefield are the same period as the Longden Common mould (fig 10); and the fragment of a bronze flat dagger found at Four Crosses, Llandysilio is also of the earliest Bronze Age, 2150-2000 BC.

Four Crosses, like Bromfield, shows the inadequacy of reliance on surface finds and the importance of aerial survey and excavation to illuminate the prehistory of the lowlands. On a gravel terrace between the Severn and Vyrnwy, only 65 metres above sea-level, fourteen ring-ditches were known by 1985 in an area comparable to the Bromfield concentration, 1500 metres by 400 metres. The excavation of eight of these showed that earlier Mesolithic activity had been followed by a Neolithic barrow inhumation about 3200 BC, with a plain Neolithic bowl crushed in the grave. The secondary Beaker inhumation and nearby pit dated about 2000 cal BC have already been mentioned. The ring-ditch of the barrow thought to succeed this Beaker activity had within it a single inhumation. Another ring-ditch surrounded only a single massive central post, showing that such ditches did not always imply burials; and offering an example of a lowland timber substitute for the standing stones of upland areas. The last phases at Four Crosses involved two barrows containing stake circles, a device thought to be restricted to larger barrows, there being six concentric stake-circles in one of the barrows here. The site also has carbon-14 dates of 1700 and 1900 cal BC for the upper filling of a ring-ditch, and pottery that has a general resemblance to some plain forms at Bromfield. It is judged to continue into the Middle Bronze Age but no later, lacking anything to compare with the Late Bronze Age material from the nearby Breidden hillfort. Iron Age and later activity there is mentioned in subsequent chapters.

North of Four Crosses at Ebnal, where the Ellesmere moraine abuts the Welsh hills, was found a small group of interesting fifteenth century bronzes. There were originally two ogival daggers of Camerton-Snowshill type and a cast flanged-axe of Arreton type, both popular forms in south-east England. One item, an end-looped spearhead is rare to the south-east but common in Early Bronze Age Ireland. The Middle and Late Bronze Age ranges from about 1400 until 600 BC. The transition about 1000 BC involved some notable technological advances, including the use of lead bronzes, but most of the later implements derive from Middle Bronze Age models.

From the Wrekin it is easy to see the significance of the Severn gorge at Buildwas as the gateway to the plain of Shrewsbury, where the Severn breaches the hill route from south Shropshire to the Pennines. Finds here include five palstaves from Preston-on-the-Weald Moors, a looped palstave from the Ercall Quarry, a spearhead from Dayhouse Moor, Cherrington, a socketed axe from Hadley and a leaf-shaped sword from the Severn at Buildwas around which place three palstaves have also been found. We meet here too the important Willowmoor bronze hoard at the foot of the Wrekin.

The area from which the hoard came has several possible barrow mounds so it may have had some long-standing religious significance: the bronzes being votive offerings deposited in the marsh. A more exciting suggestion was that they came from a Bronze Age battlefield. There were about 150 spearhead fragments, two complete spearheads, a socketed axe and some swords. A lunate spearhead places the hoard in the same general horizon as the Broadward and Guilsfield hoards, in the eighth century or later.

A trail of finds leads north via the Tern valley to the Ellesmere moraine and thence beyond Whitchurch along Cheshire's Central Ridge. In the upper Tern basin are two hoards containing socketed axes, an isolated socketed axe, a palstave and a sword. On the side of the Mersey at Ince a socketed axe was found. Between these extremes are several finds in Delamere Forest, including the Houndslow burials with three urns and a pigmy vessel, a highly ornamented cup that often accompanied urn burials. Other burials were found at Castlehill and Seven Lows, where a collared urn was recovered. Undated barrows in this area are at Galowsclough, Monarchy Hall, Tiverton and Tilstone Fearnall. South-west of this group are the barrows at Coddington and Carden Hall, while to the south-east, at Egerton Hall, were found two gold twisted bar torcs of the later Middle Bronze Age. It is likely that the ridge served both as an area of colonization and as a route from the Mersey to the middle Severn.

A second trail lies along the Severn north-westwards from the Wrekin with a palstave and looped spearhead from Wroxeter, two palstaves and a trunnion chisel from Meole Brace, a socketed axe and a palstave near Shrewsbury and then a scatter of finds along the valley of the Perry including four socketed axes, a shield, rapier and knife from Hordley, and a spearhead from Petton. At Knockin Castle a palstave was found. By way of these finds we reach a small hoard at Brogyntyn just north-west of Oswestry in the vicinity of which have been found a flanged axe, flanged chisel and four palstaves. This route will have brought us to a major break in the front of the Welsh massif, the valley of the Dee at Llangollen. Here, routes from the south-east and from north and south converge and are marked by clusters of finds, including two hoards, along the edge of the highlands. Chitty mapped no fewer than eight socketed axes along the Dee from Llangollen to Ddôl.

A similar situation may be discerned where the Severn leaves Powys for Shropshire. A socketed axe from the Breidden hillfort will have come from the Late Bronze Age occupation of the hill. Five kilometres south-west, on the hillside just above the Severn and only 100 metres from Crowther's Camp, was found a major collection of Bronze Age material: the Guilsfield hoard. It originally contained more than 120 objects dated widely through the Bronze Age; among them were a flat axe, palstaves, a looped socketed axe, a lunate spearhead, a hollow spearhead, a leaf-shaped spearhead, ferrules and fragments of leaf-shaped swords, ogival sword chapes and socketed gouges as well as partially worked and unworked bronze. It looks like the stock-in-trade of a bronze-smith and may not have been far from his work site.

North of the Vale of Llangollen a number of finds cluster around Wrexham and Mold. They include six unlooped palstaves and a chisel from Acton Park, an unlooped palstave from Buckley and a socketed knife from Minera. Early Bronze Age finds come from the plain near Holt: fragments of a food vessel, two cinerary urns and a pigmy cup. Burials on the hills of north Clwyd include a barrow at Frith y Garreg-Wen, Whitford, which yielded a dagger and food vessel sherds; six secondary cremations were inserted into the mound. At Rhydwen in the same parish a food vessel and a pigmy cup were found in a barrow, and at Bryford an Early Bronze Age cremation in an encrusted urn was accompanied by segmented blue faience beads, once thought to have been imports from Egypt but now seen to be probably made in Britain. At Lower Stables Farm, Ysceifiog, Fox excavated a ditched cairn having, in addition to its primary cremation, three secondary deposits of cremated bone, one in a cinerary urn. Barrows were often re-used.

As well as the lost gold torcs from Egerton Hall, this north-western part of our region has produced three other Bronze Age gold objects. From Mold comes a gold cape (pl 10) found in 1833 with human

Plate 10   The Mold cape of gold (Reproduced by courtesy of the Trustees of the British museum)

bones in a cist under a cairn known as Bryn-yr-Ellyon. Many amber beads were also found in the cist, presumably from the fringe of the cape. Then from Holywell comes a twisted gold bar torc similar to the Egerton Hall ones.

Dated somewhat later, perhaps around 800 BC, is a remarkable oval oak bowl with gold inlaid patterns (pl 11) recovered from a boggy field west of Caergwrle Castle. There is general agreement that the concentrically circular devices around its rim represent shields hung from the side of a boat, while a zigzag inlay near the base is taken to mark the choppy surface of the sea, towards which dip golden oars. This schematic representation seems to show knowledge of contemporary eastern Mediterranean galleys, pointing to some kind of connection with that area in our Late Bronze Age.

Only once, at Chapel Tump in Gwent, have we come across a house for the makers of all these axes and spears. This long-standing paradox of the Bronze Age, replete with burials but lacking settlements, is now partly reconciled by the recognition that hilltop settlements, defended by palisades and often succeeded by hillforts, were emerging by the Late Bronze Age, if not earlier. At present our earliest dates for these hillforts are from the northern half of the Marches, where too we have seen the greatest clustering of Late Bronze Age finds. It therefore seems appropriate to begin our next chapter in the north.

Plate 11   The Caergwrle bowl of oak with gold leaf decoration.
Height 79mm (*National Museum of Wales*)

CHAPTER SIX

The Hillforts

The hillforts are in many respects the most striking and important archaeological monuments in the Welsh border. In certain areas they occur with a density, proportionate to size, as great as anywhere in the world and display fortifications of an extent and complexity rarely surpassed in Europe. Between them they encompass a period of occupation of more than a thousand years. The general density and distribution of sites over 1.5 hectares shown on the Ordnance Survey Map of Southern Britain in the Iron Age will be substantially complete (fig 28). Nevertheless several omissions and newly discovered sites remained to be included in Hogg's invaluable British Hillforts - An index (1979) and many smaller enclosures continue to be discovered, concealed in woodland or revealed by aerial photography.

Whereas these camps were once viewed as a late reaction to the Roman invasion the chronological bracket has expanded dramatically, if uncertainly at times, to place the earliest, palisaded, sites back to the eleventh century BC, on the eve of the Late Bronze Age; and substantial ramparts were being built soon after 800 BC. Hillfort constructions thus overlap the Late Bronze and Iron Ages which may perhaps be thought of as a continuous epoch, the Hillfort period. Some sites remained in use during the Roman occupation and a few may have been occupied in the Dark Ages.

There are considerable differences in the density and size of hillforts from one part of the border to another ; and differences too in history. Foremost, after matters of date, are questions of function. Were they permanent settlements, or temporary refuges, or simply meeting places for occasional tribal gatherings? How independent were they of one another, and how extensive and permanent were the tribal territories? The kind of evidence required is difficult to obtain and often uncertain to interpret.

Our study so far has indicated that prehistoric communities often acquired objects and ideas from afar and communications seem to have been comparatively efficient. We may therefore assume that comparable tools and structures should bear comparable initial dates in neighbouring areas, permitting the construction of a relative chronology based on defensive features that can be supported by the increasing number of carbon-14 dates, even though our Hillfort period includes some of the least definitive sections of the calibration curves. It has become unfashionable to explain new phenomena by invoking invasions but we should not spurn them when other explanations seem inadequate. The pre-Roman period has migrations historically documented; in Caesar's time Britain was receiving Gaulish immigrants.

The valleys of the Dee and Weaver (fig 4)

East of the close-set Clwydian forts much of the northern border is unsuitable for hillforts; but even the limited upland areas are less intensively utilized than equivalent regions south of the Severn. North of the Ellesmere moraine the Cambrian foothills have only some seven hillforts along a front over fifty kilometres long, and four of these are close together in the valley of the Alun. The Central Ridge has a cluster of six hillforts including Eddisbury Camp and Helsby but south of Kellsboro' Castle there is only the tiny Maiden Castle, Bickerton, standing alone to control south Cheshire. North and south of the Weaver hillforts are unmapped until the scattered sites of the high Pennines are reached fifty kilometres away. The Eddisbury group therefore marks the north-eastern limit of border hillforts.

Moel y Gaer will be the place to start this review. Guilbert has shown that there was a settlement on this hillock before the rampart was built. A ring of post-holes beneath the rampart indicated a round hut of normal Bronze Age form that is assumed to be contemporary with a continuous palisade slot several metres outside the later rampart. Charcoal from the hut shows it to have been in use until at least 800 cal BC and this dating will apply also to the palisade. A palisade at the Breidden is dated 900 cal BC and one at Dinorben, Clwyd, 1075 cal BC. Eddisbury too has a pre-rampart palisade. The range of dates is near enough to indicate general contemporaneity without requiring simultaneous introduction, let alone dependence on foreign inventions. A fence is, after all, a simple and common means of delimiting a settlement, keeping stock and children in, and cattle raiders, wolves and bears at bay.

Other post-ring huts at Moel y Gaer show continued use of this form of building down to about 400 cal BC. The remodelling of the whole settlement has a carbon-14 date that would lie between about 345 and 250 cal BC. A large rampart was constructed within the line of the former palisade (fig 13). Its impressive architecture involved front posts with narrow infillings of masonry (pl 12) and apparently some horizontal timbering between these posts and a back row. The whole rampart was about six metres wide and had in front a wide irregular quarry-like ditch. This elaborate rampart is broadly within the same family of timber-laced ramparts as Eddisbury and Maiden Castle, Bickerton. Together they indicate a widespread phase of hillfort building. The dating of Maiden Castle's timbers to 390 cal BC brings the calibration for Moel y Gaer accessibly close and leaves the dates for the first timber-lacing at Dinorben, Clwyd, in early isolation at 900 cal BC. The second phase there post-dates 530 cal BC.

The post-ring huts of Moel y Gaer were replaced by a grid of four-post square huts, encouraging the view that the refortification was accompanied by radical changes in settlement, perhaps the result of folk movement. Also thought to be present are less substantial round buildings provided with door-posts as the stoutest components in a

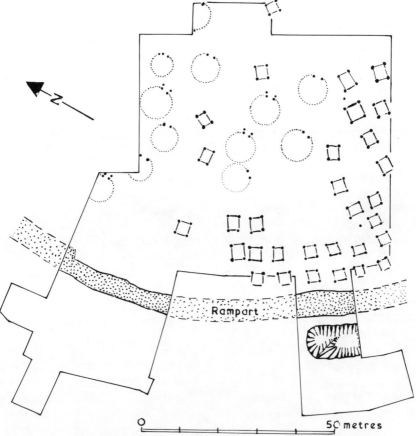

Fig 13   Sketch plan of buildings in part of Moel y Gaer, Rhosesmor,
           in phase 2, showing four-posters and stake-walled round houses,
           four of them with porch posts (After Guilbert 1975)

ring-wall of stakes, presumably with a wattle and daub covering. This settlement does not seem to have lasted long, for the four-posters were dismantled, which must have been before 100 BC at the latest, maybe before 260 BC. A somewhat shadowy re-occupation, and reconstruction of the rampart later than 180 cal BC, involved rectangular buildings with no surviving foundations or post-holes.

At some time Eddisbury Camp was provided with paired rectangular guard-rooms. Although less regular in plan, they are clearly in the Welsh border tradition of what Savory has called 'Cornovian' guard-rooms, after the tribe that occupied Shropshire. There are surface indications of guard-room recesses at Moel y Gaer too; and it may be supposed that these are contemporary with the original rampart of 345/250 cal BC and so with similar guard-rooms in the central Marches. Support for parallel development comes from the high-precision carbon-14 dates, quoted above, of 390 cal BC for Maiden Castle, Bickerton; the same date argued for major constructions in the central Marches.

Varley was convinced that the Cheshire hillforts were permanently occupied but the evidence for the duration and intensity of occupation

Plate 12   The revetment of Moel y Gaer hillfort rampart showing the stone piles between post-holes (G.C. Guilbert)

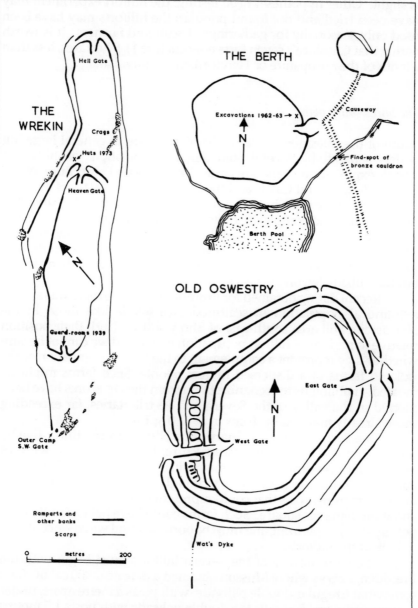

Fig 14   Three Shropshire hillforts: the Wrekin, the Berth and Old
Oswestry (adapted from Ordnance Survey plans)

is slight. Other hypotheses need testing: the hillfort experiment may have been tried and not found popular; the hillforts may have been used only seasonally for gatherings of scattered farmers. It is worth noting that Cheshire's seven forts only enclose 11.5 hectares, less than a tenth of the Shropshire or Herefordshire equivalents.

The Shrewsbury plain

South of the Ellesmere moraine the hillforts are in general large but widely separated. Several hold defensible positions on hills that permit exploitation of the lowlands, like Oliver's Point, Bury Walls, Ebury, Haughmond Castle and the Burgs. Old Oswestry is only 164 metres above the plain but what it lacks in altitude it makes up in the magnificence and complexity of its ramparts. The unusual site of the Berth, Baschurch, consists of two hillocks in a marsh connected by a causeway to the firm ground nearby. By contrast, the windswept Wrekin is at 408 metres; its uter defences may be little more than a ledge, but the hillside beyond is nearly precipitous.

Recent dating obtained for Bromfield suggests there was also an extramural population in scattered farmsteads like those in the Sharpstone Hill area south-east of Shrewsbury. Until their position relative to periods of hillfort occupation is clarified we cannot be sure whether they represent a complement to the hillfort population or the isolated farms of a dispersed hillfort people. Such farms might be moated, enabling us to recognize them from the air; scores have been plotted in the valley of the Severn and its tributaries, far exceeding those already mapped by Toms in 1973 (fig 15).

One such enclosure at Sharpstone Hill measured thirty-five by forty metres and had a four-post structure, 4.4 metres square, within a penannular eavesdrip gully ten metres in diameter. A double-ditched enclosure in the same area was strikingly similar with semicircular gullies enclosing posts that could represent elements of a four-poster about three metres square. Such farms could have held a family unit, perhaps ten people in all, and must be borne in mind while we continue to look at the hillforts.

The early history of the Severn hillforts must begin with the Breidden, Powys where Musson obtained a date near 900 cal BC for a somewhat irregular double palisade, with posts a metre apart, under a stone rampart. It recalls the double palisade with posts 1.5 metres apart under the timber-laced rampart of Ffridd Faldwyn, Montgomery. A single palisade and post-ring houses were found at Old Oswestry, where too there was Bronze Age material. The buildings inside the

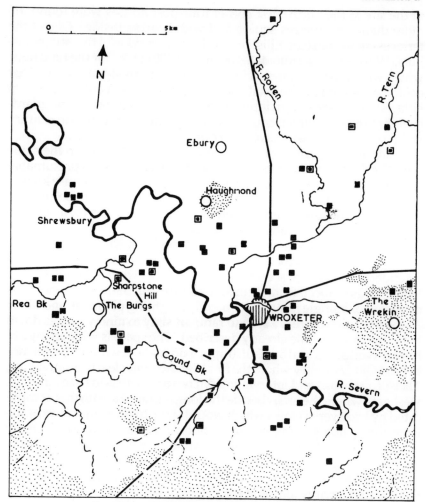

Fig 15   Rectangular enclosures in the Severn valley revealed by aerial
photography with hillforts shown by circles and land over 122
metres stippled (Extracted from a map by G.S.G.Toms, 1973)

Breidden included timber round-houses presumed to go with the
palisade, and rectangular four- and six-post huts relating to the stone
rampart and dated 360/200 cal BC, like the Moel y Gaer four-posters.
There were also stake-walled round huts along with the rectangular
buildings.

The Wrekin's first rampart was a simple dump construction on
a steep slope, enclosing about six hectares. On the most exposed part

of the site at the north-west corner four-post houses were found, no more than three metres square and with hearths inside. One of the terraces cut in the steep hillside saw the construction of five successive huts. Working back from dates of around 400 cal BC for the final huts, which were burnt, the first will have been put up about 760 BC. That could be the date for the establishment of the Wrekin outer camp. On either side of its northern inturned entrance there appear to be guard-chamber recesses which could be expected in the mid-fourth century when the last huts will have been burnt.

A shorter perimeter was then constructed higher up the slope with Cornovian guard-rooms in its southern entrance, so presumably straight after the abandonment of the lower area. No huts are known from this upper camp; nor is it known how long permanent occupation continued. The last recorded event was the burning of a corn-stack on an outer camp terrace about 90 cal AD.

It will have become clear that the hillfort earthworks we see today are the end product of centuries of use and alteration. They were extended or retracted; sometimes old defences were obliterated. The Wrekin was reduced from six to four hectares but the new defences still consisted of a single rampart, or merely a fighting platform, and ditch. At the Breidden there is a second rampart sixty to ninety metres down the slope from the one already described. The space is wide enough to have served as a corral but is also approximately as wide as the defence zone at Old Oswestry where the final defence was clearly multivallate. There, four banks and intervening ditches are increased to seven at the west gate where the areas beside the long entrance are further compli-cated by transverse banks which would serve to trap anyone escaping from the killing ground of the corridor. This is the most northerly example of the developed multivallation that occurs spasmodically between Shropshire and Dorset, and must belong to the later years of the Iron Age. Very few hillforts exhibit such extensive corrugation of terrain, presumably aimed at holding the enemy about ninety metres away from the main rampart. It may be related to sling warfare, as argued by Wheeler for Maiden Castle, Dorset; but was perhaps more likely designed to outrange spear-thrown firebrands, since sling-stones are a rare occurrence in the Marches.

The central Marches (fig 3, p 5)

This area contains the greatest variety of hillforts. The mountain-top eyrie of Caer Caradoc by Church Stretton, is an ideal example, one might think, of a hillfort refuge. Yet this uncomfortable enclosure

Plate 13   Titterstone Clee hillfort rampart of dolerite blocks

has within it numerous hut platforms, and its inturned entrance with guard-room recesses is approached by a graded path cut obliquely into the hillside. Caer Caradoc must have been a permanent settlement.

With this in mind we might turn to Titterstone Clee, where a ruined stone rampart sprawls across the moor, encompassing originally more than twenty-eight hectares (pl 13). It was thus three times as large as any other hillfort in the central Marches, equal to the Breidden but surpassed by Llanymynech which is twice the size of either. On grounds of size and siting on particularly imposing hills such sites must be reckoned to have had a special role but there is no evidence to distinguish the function of Titterstone Clee Camp from that of any other hillfort. O'Neil's excavations were mainly concerned with the defences that were going to be quarried and he showed that a timber wall had fronted the rampart before the existing stone revetment was built. More than one period was involved at the South Gate where paired rectangular Cornovian guard-rooms stood behind the twin portals. Titterstone Clee was therefore at least partly contemporary with the Wrekin and the Roveries where Thomas re-excavated twin guard-rooms of similar form. No Iron Age or Roman material came from either Titterstone Clee or the Roveries.

A site holding important evidence for early hillfort activity is Caynham Camp near Ludlow which yielded unstratified sherds of two vessels tempered with dolerite (fig 17), the nearest outcrop of which is four kilometres away. Caynham was apparently being supplied from the same area that provided the urns for the Bronze Age cemetery at Bromfield and later for the Iron Age farmers there. One of the Caynham pots could be loosely compared with pots of either period at Bromfield but Gelling's comparison with pot 6 on fig 12, now dated 870 cal BC, remains the best. The parallel may be close enough to hint that Caynham had a Late Bronze Age occupation. A palisade, such as might be expected as early as that, was not clearly proven at Caynham where the first rampart was apparently strengthened with horizontal timbers, like Maiden Castle, Bickerton. A date of about 390 cal BC date for charred wood from this rampart makes it a likely contemporary of the timber-laced Maiden Castle, Bickerton rampart of 390 cal BC. The firing of this rampart may denote local hostilities, with neighbours or with invading tribes from far afield.

In front of the degraded remains of the burnt Caynham rampart a small bank was built, possibly with a crude stone revetment at the front and a stockade on top. A massive rampart was later built, partly from internal quarrying, over the earlier works. About then, or possibly a little later, a deeply inturned entrance was constructed that must be expected to contain guard-rooms. The duration and nature

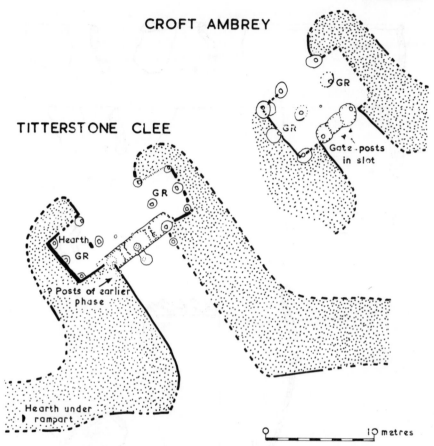

CROFT AMBREY

TITTERSTONE CLEE

Fig 16 Guard-room phase gates at Croft Ambrey and Titterstone Clee Hill.
Croft Ambrey, south-west gate period VA (based on Stanford 1974,
fig 16); Titterstone Clee, main entrance period III (based on
O'Neil 1934, pl X with the period I & II gate slot added)

of the subsequent occupation remains unknown, though excavations
in the entrance hinted at a complexity of features and some of the
pottery looks typologically late.

On the sloping interior at Caynham was a terrace with a slot for
the wall of a semicircular building, eight metres in diameter with
several large posts across the front (fig 18). It presumably belongs to the
hillfort occupation and the lack of parallels indicates an unusual
function, perhaps as a temple. The same area had numerous post-holes
that probably included at least two four-post huts. Even small trenches
usually exposed post-holes, often recut many times. It looks certain

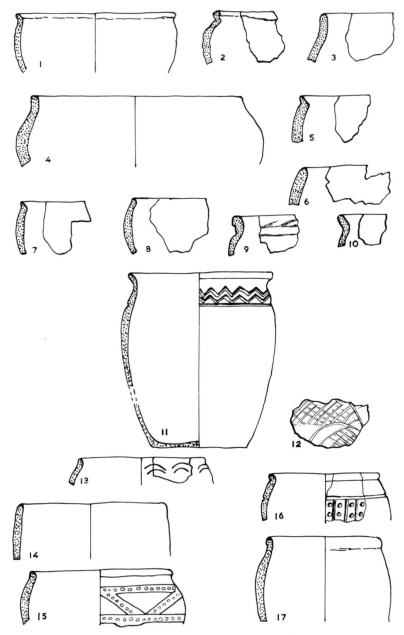

Fig 17 Hillfort pottery x1/4, 1-3 the Wrekin; 4-6 the Breidden;
7-10 Caynham; 11-14 Llanmelin Wood; 15-17 Lydney Park

that a close cover of buildings persisted over a very long period. Quantities of carbonized wheat and the charred stumps of the posts themselves were found in several post-holes. The end posts of the semicircular building were burnt; and so were the two western posts of the four-poster that lay across the west side of this building. Could one of these fires relate to the burning of the timber-laced rampart? and the other to the Roman conquest?

The wheat from Caynham is important evidence for the use, and presumably the growing, of wheat in the Marches. Its presence in numerous post-holes that cannot all be contemporary suggests it was in everyday use. Two samples of carbonized wheat from the Wrekin were dated 760/530 cal BC and 90 cal AD. Between them these finds suggest that wheat was probably grown throughout the Hillfort period.

Only at Caynham so far, late pottery permits speculation that the hillforts of this sector remained occupied after the early fourth-century construction of large ramparts, inturned entrances and guard-rooms. The clearance of conifers at Bury Ditches has made possible a reassessment of the defence sequence there. The inner rampart, with guard-room recesses apparent in the entrance corridor was succeeded on one half of the circuit by a larger rampart built outside. This is another site that therefore has a longer history though not, as I previously thought, with developed multivallation.

The density of hillforts in these central hills is greater than to the north, with more evidence for long-continued use in Shropshire and Powys than in Cheshire and Clwyd. Hillfort settlement was clearly better suited to the social and economic needs of the hill tribes than to those of the people of the northern plains. The central hills contain not only several large hillforts but also a sprinkling of the smaller ones that are commoner on the sides of the Welsh valleys. Guilbert regarded the earthworks on Stitt Hill and Ratlinghope Hill on the Long Mynd as non-hillfort enclosures related to nearby cross-dykes, indicating a possible Bronze Age origin as argued for comparable plateau sites in southern England.

It remains to be seen whether the tiny hillforts of south-west Shropshire - places like Wart Hill and the outpost by the Roveries - were continually occupied or only represent a phase in which units of only half a hectare were preferred. They surely had a different status from the even smaller enclosures like Bromfield (fig 19) which extend the Severn valley ditched farmsteads to the county's southern limits. Bromfield is now shown by carbon-14 dating and Morris's analysis of the pottery to be Iron Age. With only two four-posters, the smaller probably a granary, some haytrees, racks and shallow clay-lined retting or boiling tanks, it would have been just a family unit.

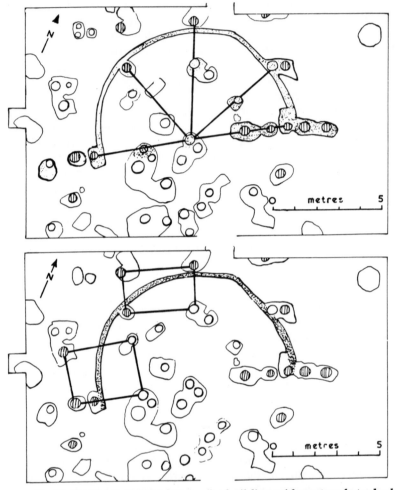

Fig 18 Caynham Camp semicircular building with post-sockets shaded.
Above as in Gelling 1962-3 with extended facade and main
rafters shown and its slot and post-holes stippled.
Below An alternative with two four-posters superimposed.
Both reconstructions leave many unexplained post-holes

The farm seems to have been brought into the ditched enclosure,
possibly in the third century BC, after a period as an open site. Within
a hundred years the huts were disused and new ones built outside,
while the enclosure was still used for cooking with boiling stones. Iron-
working continued just outside the ditch. Such sites may have been
complementary to hillforts or periodic alternatives.

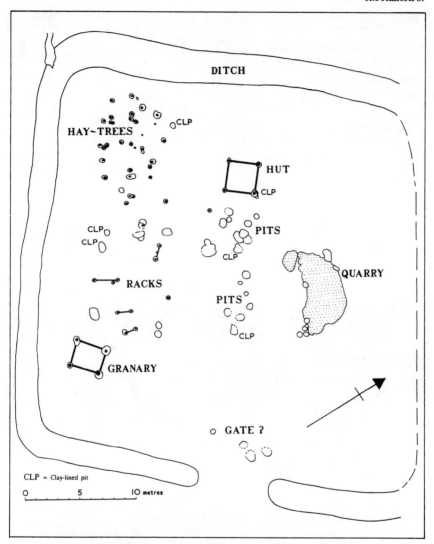

DITCH

HAY-TREES
CLP

HUT
CLP

CLP
CLP
PITS

CLP
QUARRY
RACKS
PITS
CLP

GRANARY

GATE ?

CLP = Clay-lined pit

0   5   10 metres

Fig 19   **The Iron Age farm at Bromfield**

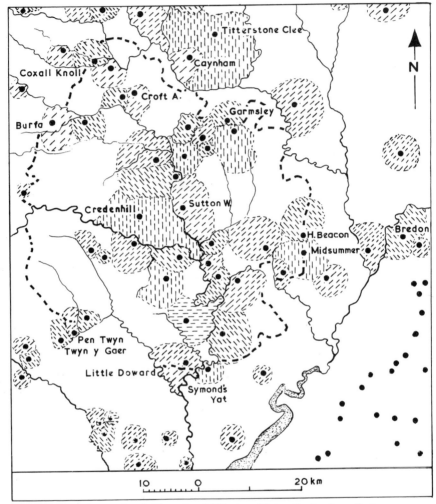

Fig 20 Decangian and neighbouring hillforts with territories in ratio to
enclosed areas. The Herefordshire boundary is pecked and dots mark
Cotswolds hillforts. (Based on Stanford 1972 with modifications)

The Herefordshire basin

Cultural and political boundaries do not necessarily follow the dictates
of topography but there is a strong case for believing that the tribal
boundaries of the Iron Age enclosed the same geographical region as
did the historic county of Herefordshire. This is an area where half the
camps are over six hectares and normally furnished with big ramparts.

Central to it is the largest member, Credenhill Camp, enclosing twenty hectares and twice as large as its nearest Herefordshire contender, Sutton Walls. Its position in the geographical centre, close to where Roman Kenchester and Saxon Hereford later stood, supports its claim to be the hillfort capital of this tribe. It is difficult to know what kind of evidence would be compelling for proving a capital function; certainly the limited rescue excavation at Credenhill produced nothing exceptional. Before returning to that we may extend our view to the perimeter and notice that there are several large hillforts beside the old county boundary (fig 20): Burfa Camp in Powys, Garmsley in Worcestershire, Herefordshire Beacon and Midsummer Hill in Herefordshire, Symonds Yat Camp in Gloucestershire and the Little Doward Camp in Herefordshire. In adddition, Pen Twyn is only one kilometre inside Gwent.

In Herefordshire there is a remarkably consistent pattern of structural and artefactual material. This is especially so for Croft Ambrey, Midsummer Hill and Credenhill where there are similarities in defence, houses and pottery to support their inclusion in the same cultural groups, at least from the early fourth century BC. Although less specific, the pottery and defences of Sutton Walls, Poston Camp, Dinedor Camp and Aconbury Camp bring them in too. Early gateway plans at Twyn y Gaer, Gwent are similar to the Herefordshire sequence and at that time the hillfort was being supplied with pottery from the Malvern Hills area. In later years, pottery of a more southern aspect may show a change of allegiance to the Silures of South Wales.

Capler Camp alone of the area's excavated hillforts has no evidence of permanent occupation; but local circumstances probably influenced Jack's 1924 conclusions. The hill is Old Red Sandstone, with acid soil that dissolves pottery, metal and bone. Moreover, in the 1920's expectations within hillforts were shadowy indeed; and excavation was with long narrow trenches which gave the professional labourers little chance of recognizing post-holes. It seems best therefore to regard the conclusions from Capler as inconclusive rather than negative.

For the rest, the hillfort story seems to begin in the sixth century, the new carbon-14 calibration matching the 1974 Croft Ambrey dating rather than the Midsummer Hill 1981 chronology, which was revised to Clark's calibration. The first rampart at Croft Ambrey was set on clean turf, showing this to be a new settlement. The defensive ditch, only 1.2 metres deep, was inadequate to provide the rampart which must have received additional spoil from small internal terraces prepared for huts (fig 21). These were four-posters, set out in lines to which most of those excavated adhered throughout the long occupation. After their initial emplacement some were rebuilt as many as six times

PERIOD I — 7th century B.C.

Quarry scoop
Rampart
Ditch

PERIOD IV — 5th century B.C.

Demolished rampart
Quarry-ditch

PERIOD VII — 1st century B.C.

Storage pit

0   20 metres   Recut ditch   Counterscarp bank

Fig 21 Restored profiles of Croft Ambrey's defences (Stanford 1974a, fig 11)

with all posts set within half a metre of the original locations (fig 22).

The excavated area was small but included a variety of terrain. Similar buildings were found on the steepest slope, 1:7, on top of the hill at 305 metres and on the largest area of flat ground beside the West Gate. Even small trenches, as at Caynham, usually picked up part of a post-hole complex. The topographical variety and repeated renewal confirms a contrast with sites like Moel y Gaer and leads us to think that most of the main camp of Croft Ambrey was covered by rows of buildings separated by narrow paths.

These huts, ranging from 1.8 to 3.6 metres square, are similar to those at the Breidden, Moel y Gaer and the Wrekin where four-posters were also more or less square. Hearths were found in four at the Wrekin and one or two at Croft Ambrey had patches of burnt bedrock. Since hearths would normally be in houses it seems that about half of these building were dwellings. The others, and certainly the small ones, would have served as granaries or stores for other things.

The early inhabitants of Croft Ambrey left no pottery behind; and

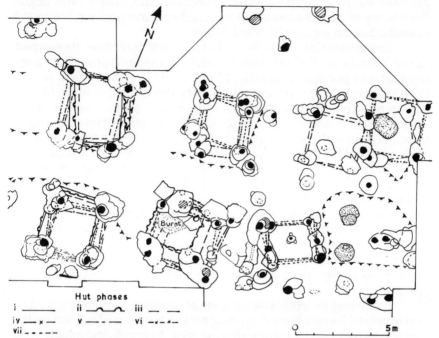

Hut phases
i _____ ii ⌒⌒ iii ____
iv __x__ v __.__ vi __.-..__
vii _.___

5 m

Fig 22 Rebuilt huts at Croft Ambrey. Surviving post-sockets solid black; pits stippled (After Stanford 1974a figs 50 and 51)

none found on the site need date before the enlargement of the camp in about 390 BC. Morris has shown that the occasional dolerite-tempered sherds are Iron Age, and not a Bromfield Bronze Age distribution.

Nowhere in Herefordshire is there evidence of prehistoric timber-laced or timber-framed ramparts. The only possible pre-earthwork palisade evidence is a single post-hole at Sutton Walls. It is therefore likely that this area was not entered until the seventh century and that there was a great expansion of settlement in the early fourth. In north-west Gwent, a fenced enclosure at Twyn y Gaer hillfort, is dated about 390 cal BC - the same as Maiden Castle Bickerton, Croft Ambrey IV and Midsummer I, the latter dated by small twigs on the rampart-quarry floor.

The introduction of new ideas at this time, when the Celts under Brennus were storming over the Alps to assault Rome, is indicated by the construction of small sub-rectangular timber guard-rooms in the new inturned entrance of Midsummer Hill Camp. Although alone so far in the Marches, except possibly at Credenhill, the Midsummer gateway was probably paralleled at Maiden Castle, Dorset. Now began the history of guard-rooms and inturned entrances which are found from the Severn estuary to North Wales.

Credenhill Camp is believed to have been built now, its rampart raised from the spoil of an internal quarry. At the same time a new large rampart was put up outside the old circuit at Croft Ambrey in period IV. It was raised from an enormous quarry-ditch to provide a bank that still stands five metres above its old ground surface and is some seventeen metres wide at the base (fig 21). The inhabitants continued for some time with the old square buildings and, unlike contemporary Midsummer Hill, had no timber guard-rooms. Within the century, however, both Croft Ambrey and Midsummer Hill were provided with stone-and-timber guard-rooms like those of the Shropshire and Cheshire hillforts. The contemporary gate at Twyn y Gaer had no guard-rooms but utilized a slot across the corridor in the same way as Croft Ambrey and Midsummer Hill. Neither the transverse slot nor the guard-rooms were used in any subsequent period, so these gates should be structural parallels of the period 390-262 BC. Around 390 BC all four sites were using pottery made somewhere near the Malvern Hills.

Following Peacock's recognition of commercial pottery distribution several different manufacturing areas have been identified on the basis of the rock used for tempering the grog. In pots found mostly west of the Malverns the Group B1 potters included fragments of limestone, probably of Silurian age. Their wares were normally stamped with a single, or occasionally double, line of arrowheads or chevrons, S-stamps or zigzags (fig 23) usually between two tooled grooves near the rim of barrel-shaped jars or bowls. Soot encrustations in the hollow stamps show they were cooking pots.

Morris has shown that what were once thought to be vesicular B1 wares are tempered with mudstone, forming Group D. They are also normally stamped, often less crisply, and are dominant from Midsummer Hill to the Cotswolds. Another firm, Group A, had Malvernian rock in their grog. Although they also used some stamped decoration, they more commonly relied on linear-tooled patterns, simple trellis designs or crescents like finger-nail impressions. In the early years their pots were comparable in form and internal rim grooving with Groups B1 and D but simpler rims and careless decoration ensued. Yet it was this Group A who penetrated the western markets, perhaps from the fourth century BC but with increased effect during the first. By the end of the Iron Age they had ousted Group B1 from the Marches.

A minor Group C, with designs similar to those of Group A, incorporated sandstone, probably from the Cowleigh Park beds just west of the

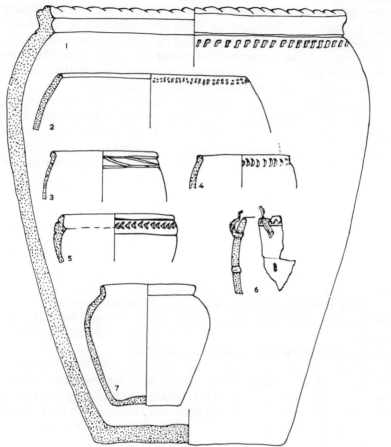

Fig 23 Iron Age pottery made near the Malverns, from Sutton Walls (1) and Croft Ambrey, with an iron repair on 6. Approximately x1/4

Malverns. Coming into production in the late Iron Age, they produced saucepan pots with thickened rims and linear-tooled designs that were still on sale in the early Roman period. Another minor group of poor potters used material with dolerite, supplying sites within about twenty kilometres of Titterstone Clee Hill.

Most of the pots of Groups A, B1 and D that went westwards were sold within or close to the historic boundary of Herefordshire, although occasionally they went as far as Aberystwyth and the Brenig valley, Clwyd. Croft Ambrey was their most northerly regular customer and pots there were sometimes repaired with iron dogs to save waiting for the potter to come round again. There was much stamped pottery at Poston Camp and it was present in the fourth century at Twyn y Gaer. In the heart of Decangian territory it was used at Credenhill, Sutton Walls, Dinedor and Aconbury. The competence of the potting and the occurrence of stamped motifs in north-western France in the fifth and fourth centuries makes it likely that there was initially some connection between the two traditions.

At the same time as these potters started there was reorganization of hillforts with some new foundations. A few were enlarged from under four to eight hectares; and whereas the earlier enclosures had simple gap entrances, their extensions have markedly inturned forms. Hillforts that were enlarged in this way - conjecturally when inturned entrances were introduced with timber guard-rooms about 390 BC - are the Herefordshire Beacon, Ivington Camp, Wall Hills Ledbury and the Little Doward Camp (fig 24). Other sites of 6.5-10.5 hectares that may have been established now are Aconbury, Eaton, Gaer Cop, Oldbury, Chase Wood, Wall Hills Thornbury, Sutton Walls and Dinmore Hill. Not all early hillforts need have been under four hectares but a marked preference for large units is clear after 390 BC. Credenhill was set out now and so too was the eight-hectare enclosure of Midsummer Hill.

This interpretation must involve either the swarming of scattered farmers into hillforts, or the uniting of small hillforts, or an infusion of new settlers. The arguments adduced for the late penetration of the Herefordshire basin make it attractive as the scene of one of the last major acts of colonization in lowland Britain before the English settlement. Other pointers to the arrival of new people are the huts at Credenhill and Midsummer Hill which were oblong four-posters about 3.6 by 2.4 metres. This contrasts with the squarish forms at Croft Ambrey and sites further north in the Marches. Four-posters earlier than 390 BC elsewhere in Britain are also square.

Post-holes at Credenhill show that the huts were rebuilt several times but had no trace of hearths; they probably had raised wooden floors. Standing only three metres apart, they were in rows beside five-metre streets giving a density comparable with Croft Ambrey.

Midsummer Hill has hut terraces on gradients up to one in three, surveyed first by Lines in 1870; and again in 1965. The two surveys concur in showing about 230 terraces where vegetation permitted detailed observations (fig 25). Excavations in 1969-70, in a flat area on

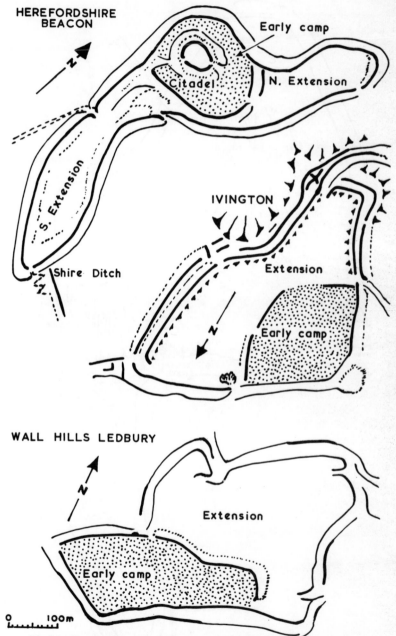

Fig 24 Three enlarged Herefordshire hillforts. Scale the same as in fig 14. Based on the plans of the RCHM

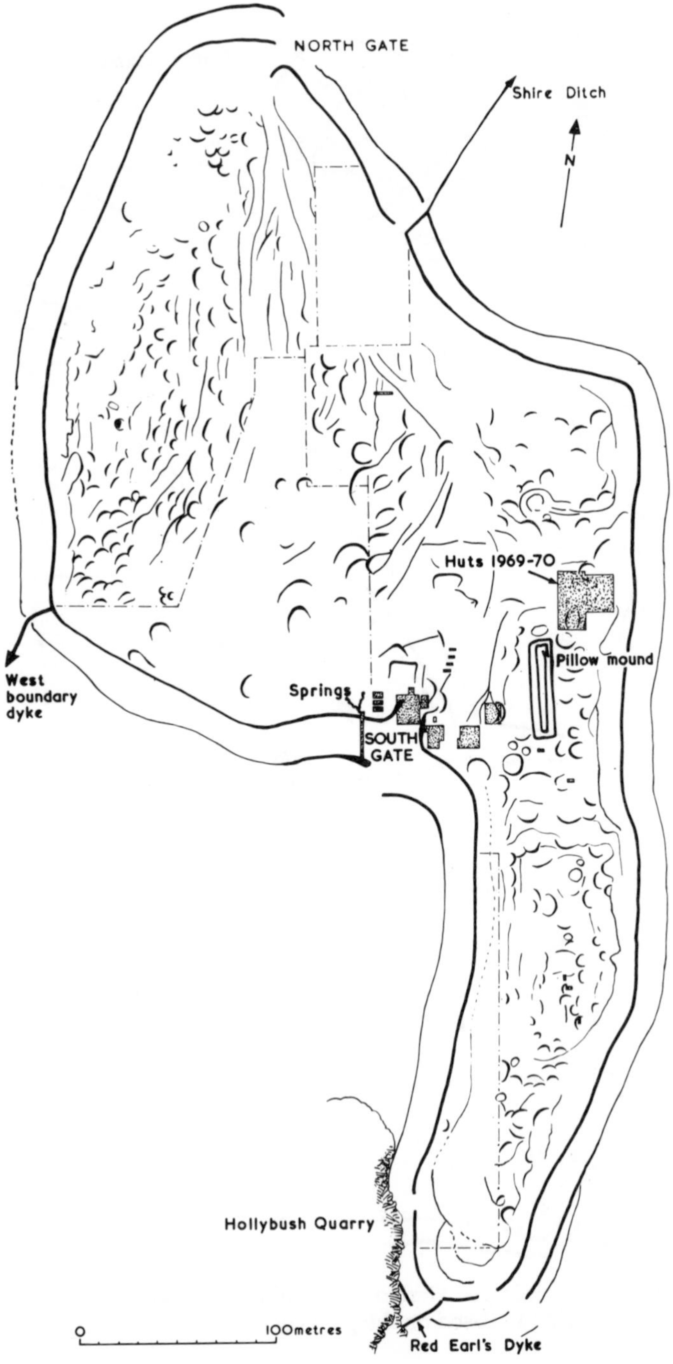

NORTH GATE

Shire Ditch

N

Huts 1969-70

Pillow mound

West
boundary
dyke

Springs

SOUTH
GATE

Hollybush Quarry

0   100metres

Red Earl's Dyke

the Hollybush side of the camp where no terraces were apparent, showed that four-posters of Credenhill shape were close-set and repeatedly rebuilt. Originally 3.6 by 2.4 metres, they tended to become square with later reconstruction. There was however very little movement of huts from the original sites which were 4.5 metres apart in both directions; but late infilling reduced this. Of the nine buildings explored here, burnt sub-hearth areas survived in five, confirming the view that roughly half were dwellings. Adding this evidence to that of the terraces it is clear that the hillfort was virtually covered by huts, leaving little space for other activities save in the narrow quarry scoops behind the rampart.

In assessing Herefordshire's Iron Age population it will be assumed that much the same building densities prevailed on all hillforts, none of which show evidence of different house types. Assuming that every other hut at Croft Ambrey was a dwelling for four people, the population within the main camp ramparts would have been between 180 and 240 per hectare, appreciably higher than has been estimated for some hillforts elsewhere in Britain. Using the lower estimate the total population of the Herefordshire hillforts would have been about 25,000. The overall density of twelve persons per square kilometre may be compared with an estimate of nine for Domesday Herefordshire and twelve, once more, calculated from the 1377 Poll Tax returns. With the exception of a farm ditch and an incompletely circular structure underlying the Roman villa at Kenchester, there is no dated evidence of extramural settlement to swell these estimates.

If the same figures are used for Shropshire the hillfort population would be about 18,000. The hut samples on the Wrekin and Caynham support this, but the results of limited excavations at Ebury and Burrow Camps were negative. We have already seen that there is a much larger, unquantified, extramural potential in that county.

Despite their uncertainties, such estimates raise the possibility that the population in both counties peaked in the Iron Age, declined under the Romans and only recovered by the late Middle Ages. They make it clear that by the end of the Iron Age large areas must have been clear of trees and used for farming.

We cannot know the balance between arable and pastoral production, though geography would favour pastoralism in the north and on high ground everywhere. Storage-pits, as found in southern England, have been presumed by some to be essential concomitants of

Fig 25 Plan of Midsummer Hill Camp showing presumed hut terraces and other breaks of slope. 1969-70 excavations stippled. Limits of detailed survey shown by broken lines (Simplified from Stanford 1981)

large-scale arable farming in Iron Age Britain; yet, while carbonized grain is common as far north as the Wrekin, pits have only been found at Sutton Walls, Credenhill and Croft Ambrey. Even then they are very small and late in the Iron Age. Grain was mostly stored in four-post granaries measuring up to 2.4 by 2.0 metres; the damper climate and less porous soils made general reliance on deep storage pits impracticable.

Climate may also explain the predominance of wheat at Caynham, Croft Ambrey and Midsummer Hill whereas elsewhere in southern Britain barley has also been important. The corn was mainly ground on saddle querns, though rotaries as well appeared at Twyn y Gaer. Salt from Droitwich and Cheshire was brought in disposable clay vases that I formerly thought were crude field ovens. Droitwich distributed its product from the Severn estuary to Sharpstone Hill, monopolizing Herefordshire in the early days but with increased competition from Cheshire later. Fig 26 shows other items of Iron Age equipment.

At Croft Ambrey bones of cattle, sheep and swine were present in almost equal numbers whereas at Sutton Walls cattle accounted for half, sheep for a third and swine for a sixth. Croft Ambrey's high proportion of swine may reflect more forest for pannage, or a distinct dietary tradition, or the use of pigs to break new ground or serve as substitute ploughs. The Whitehouses' study of the Croft Ambrey bones showed that a majority of all animals were over-wintered at least once; the rarity of immature sheep may indicate breeding for wool.

Forest clearance would have been a slow process caused mainly by grazing preventing regeneration, and with ring-barking and pigs playing a larger part than clear-felling. Slowly flocks could have increased or been concentrated in areas that were more convenient for supervision. Any extension of the arable area would have increased productivity per hectare and made even more pasture superfluous. Such a process might theoretically enable early hillforts to concentrate more on the nearest land and free distant pastures for new settlers.

With a thinning forest, any large demand for structural timber would clear large trees over a wide area. This would happen when a new hillfort was established, particularly if it was to have a timber-laced rampart. The renewal of palisades, fences and huts, and the demands of hearth and forge, were insistent demands on the forest.

Four hillforts (fig 27) have defences that merit special regard. First comes Wapley Camp, on the top of an escarpment, with five banks on the east side where the slope is negligible, but only four on the steeper slope west of the South Gate. At their widest they extend over ninety metres like those of Old Oswestry and the entrance itself is one of our finest with a ninety-metre passage that turns left at the top towards a hidden gate. Wapley's close rival in earthwork is Risbury

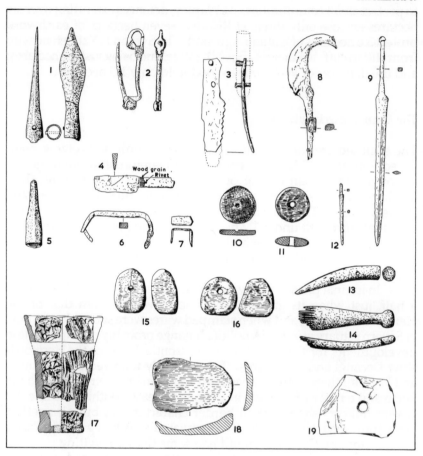

Fig 26 Iron Age equipment from Croft Ambrey and Sutton Walls (13 and 14)
Iron: 1 Spearhead; 2 Brooch; 3 Saw; 4 Knife; 5 Ox goad;
6 & 7 Dogs; 8 Sickle; 9 Dagger; 12 Awl
Stone: 10 Disc; 11 Spindle whorl; 18 Saddle quern; 19 Thatch weight
Antler: 13 Cheek-piece.   Bone: 14 Weaving comb
Baked clay: 15 & 16 Loom weights; 17 Salt container

Scales: 1-7 x1/3 8-14 x1/6 15-16 x1/12 17 x1/9 18-19 x1/24

Camp, remarkable for its low siting on a hillock by a marsh overlooked at a distance by higher ground. On the flat east side are four or five banks and ditches spread over ninety metres. By contrast this defence zone narrows to seventy-three metres on the steep western side where the entrance was located. Such vast work was undertaken just to protect small communities. At Wapley, defences extending over six hectares enclose only three; at Risbury, seven hectares of earthwork protect 3.6 hectares of habitable ground. The Symonds Yat defences go from cliff to cliff, 106 metres above the Wye, enclosing just 2.6 hectares; and the defences of Welshbury Wood hold only 1.3 hectares.

The Dean-Trelleck uplands

The enclosed area of the hillforts of Gwent is only 43 hectares, compared with the 138 hectares enclosed in Herefordshire hillforts. So although the Roman capital of the Silures was at Caerwent, their territory must have extended far to the west for them to have resisted Rome so long. The commonest element across south Wales is the univallate fort with under 1.2 hectares enclosed but south Gwent has six sites enclosing 2 hectares and several multivallate defences. Of the latter, only the south-east defences of Lodge Wood approach ninety metres.

In its final phase Twyn y Gaer was reduced from two hectares to a half, just when its gateway sequence diverged from that of the Herefordshire forts, and when stamped wares were succeeded by pots of Severn estuary affinity. A political change probably prompted these developments, for Twyn y Gaer is at the frontier between the Herefordshire Decangi and the Silures. This probably followed the Monnow and Wye, for there is an undeveloped zone, ten kilometres wide, to the north and a rarity of hillforts in Dean to the east. Within this line the Gwent hillforts share certain border characteristics but also reflect other traditions. None of the five excavated sites had a timber-laced rampart though Coed y Bwnydd had some timber revetting.

At Twyn y Gaer (fig 29), following the use of a fenced enclosure of about 395 cal BC, an inturned entrance was built with a slot across the gate position. There are inturned entrances east of the Wye at Spital Meend and Lydney Park; and in Gwent at Twyn Bell and Llanmelin Wood. Twyn y Gaer had no guard-rooms but post-holes under the north Llanmelin inturn may denote them there.

A frequent feature in border hillforts is an internal quarry-ditch to build ramparts, and this has been found at Llanmelin Wood, Sudbrook, Lydney Park and Coed y Bwnydd. At the last-named site two radiocarbon dates close to 400 cal BC were obtained for timber from a round house over a silted quarry scoop. Twyn y Gaer also had round houses, probably turf-walled with two door posts.

Apart from the stamped wares already discussed from Twyn y Gaer, the contemporary pottery from these southern sites, formerly called

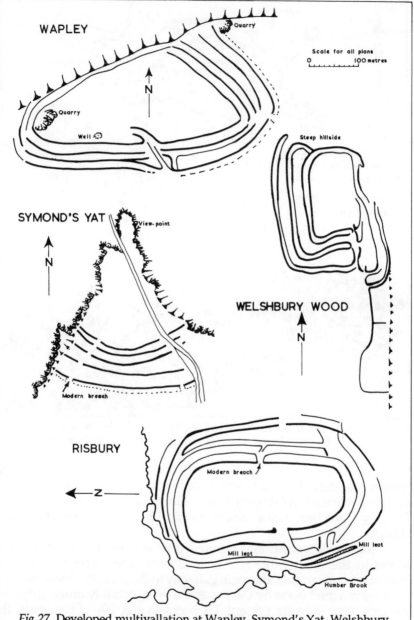

Fig 27 Developed multivallation at Wapley, Symond's Yat, Welshbury Wood and Risbury camps. Scale as on figures 14 and 24. Based on Ordnance Survey and RCHM plans

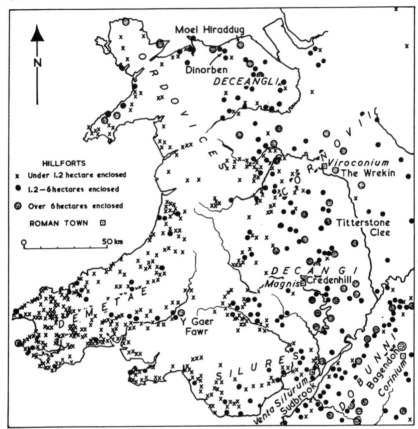

Fig 28 Hillforts and tribes in Wales and the Marches (Hillforts as on
Map of S.Britain in the Iron Age with additions in the Marches)

Iron Age B, has general affinities with Glastonbury wares across the
Severn. Most are plain jars with simple rounded or bead-rims, while
the few decorated sherds from Llanmelin, Sudbrook, Lydney Park and
Twyn y Gaer bear Glastonbury motifs like incised eyebrows and
zigzags.

Sudbrook's position as a route centre, with ferry connections and
access to the main ridge routes of Gwent, must have made it an
important trading post, the main gateway to the area. Its defences have
been encroached upon by the sea and it was probably much larger in
the Iron Age than its present 1.4 hectares (fig 29). Size apart, its
attributes are those of a capital hillfort, forerunner to Caerwent. A
massive rampart, 5.2 metres high and 15 metres wide, used spoil from
both quarry and defensive ditches and incorporated deposits of occupat-

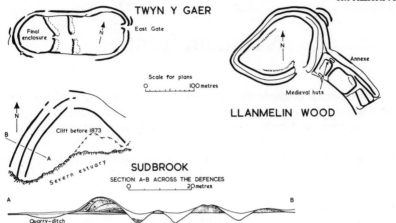

Fig 29 Hillfort varieties in Gwent: Simplified plans of Twyn y Gaer (after Probert 1976), Llanmelin Wood and Sudbrook (after Nash-Williams 1933 and 1939). Scale as for figures 14, 24 and 27

ion soil from pre-rampart activity. The defences eventually included three ditches with accompanying banks in addition to the main rampart and extended over 58 metres from the rampart crest. In the early Roman period pits were dug through trodden surfaces in the quarry-ditch and as a result Roman coins and pottery were recovered at very low levels in excavations too narrow to allow proper appreciation of the stratification.

Probably to be associated with Manning's suggested Roman use of the site as a supply depot are numerous wheel-turned Iron Age sherds comparable with pots of the latest Iron Age on the Cotswolds. Against the former view that they represent an Iron Age C invasion, is the rarity of British coins. Along with the rest of the Marches, Gwent lay beyond the main influence of the coin-using Dobunni, whose few coins in Gwent probably came in with Roman soldiers. There are gold staters of Catti from Chepstow and Anted from Dingestow and Chepstow, carrying on the obverse the branched emblem that is peculiar to Dobunnic staters and on the reverse a schematized triple-tailed horse. A gold stater of Corio from 'Llanthony Abbey,' may have come from, or via, the sister abbey, of the same name, by Gloucester. Two uninscribed Dobunnic coins come from the Forest of Dean.

To understand the hillforts of Gwent we need two or three detailed accounts comparable to that from Probert's excavations at Twyn y Gaer. Then we might learn whether Gwent was a springboard for ideas coming into the Marches or whether it was largely isolated by the forest from outside influences.

CHAPTER SEVEN

A Roman frontier

The prehistoric organization of society and economy is likely to have been achieved within the range of visibility of our chosen viewpoints, since regional self-sufficiency was the prime requirement. Under the Romans local individuality was subordinated to the requirements of an Imperial frontier; so we will abandon the regional subdivisions and view the border as a whole through the eyes of the invaders (fig 30).

Although now in the historic period, little can be known without archaeological discovery, for the surviving passages of written history are few and generalized. The archaeological and historical evidence must be married to offer a reasonable interpretation of both records. The changes in interpretation over the years are more easily understood when it is remembered that Tacitus' account of the conquest of this part of Britain is not only incomplete but lacks accompanying maps. The only geographical locations he mentions are the river Severn and the tribal territories of the Silures, Decangi (possibly meaning Deceangli) and the Ordovices.

The Roman invasion of Britain in AD 43 led quickly to the defeat of the British forces in the south-east. After his brother Togodumnus had been killed in the battle on the Thames, Caratacus fled west. By AD 47 a frontier had been established roughly along the Jurassic escarpment, the subsequent line of the Fosse Way. Legio II Augusta was eventually to establish a fortress at Exeter, and Legio IX Hispana one at Lincoln. Somewhere between the two, the Midlands would have been under the control of Legio XIV Gemina, who were eventually to appear at Wroxeter. The years following the Thames battle saw the reduction of at least twenty hillforts in southern Britain by Legio II under Vespasian, hillforts that included places like the multivallate Maiden Castle, Dorset. This may be the context in which similar defensive techniques were introduced at Old Oswestry, Wapley, Risbury, Symonds Yat, Welshbury Wood and Lodge Wood camps. A counter argument is that refugees from vanquished hillforts would have been poor sponsors to promote a failed system to those who yet remained free. Perhaps in both areas developed multivallation reflects the partial success of professional military architects before the Roman invasion.

In the winter of AD 47-48, when the governor Aulus Plautius was replaced by Ostorius Scapula, tribes from outside the occupied part of Britain invaded the Roman province so that when Scapula arrived he had first to regain control of some of the frontier districts. Having done this and even disarmed some of Rome's British allies, he attacked a tribe recorded by Tacitus as the Decangi. The identification of this tribe and its territory affects our opinions on both the course of the Roman conquest and the pre-Roman tribal division of the Marches. Several regions may be eliminated on the strength of inscriptional evidence for other tribes (fig 28). To the south-east, at Cirencester, was Corinium Dobunnorum, Roman capital of the Dobunni, while to the south the Silures had their capital at Caerwent - Venta Silurum. To the north the Cornovii are commemorated in an inscription over the forum of their capital at Wroxeter - Viroconium Cornoviorum. The tribe in Clwyd, though lacking a known Roman capital, are recorded as the Deceangli on numerous pigs of lead found in Clwyd and further afield. Because of the similarity of name they are generally assumed to be the people Tacitus called 'Decangi'. We cannot put bounds to any of these territories nor to that of the Ordovices who occupied north-west Wales and possibly extended into Powys.

The one major area left is Herefordshire where the only relevant inscription is on a milestone of Numerian's reign discovered in Kenchester's town wall. This is inscribed with a much eroded 'RPCD', usually assumed to stand for Res Publica Civitatis Dobunnorum, and to indicate that in the third century AD this was Dobunnic territory.

Because of the considerable archaeological differences between Herefordshire, where no coins or wheel-turned pottery were used before the Roman conquest, and the Dobunnic area with its own coins, wheel-turned pottery and new-style valley settlements like Bagendon, it is difficult to accept that the two regions were united before the Roman conquest. An alternative allocation of Herefordshire to the Silures meets with comparable archaeological contrasts: in hillfort size and density as well as pottery and huts. If Herefordshire was neither Dobunnic nor Silurian it would be strange for it to have passed unnoticed in the story of the conquest. It seems simpler to assume that its people were indeed the Decangi of whom Tacitus wrote, whether or not the D on the milestone stood for Decangi or Dobunni.

The similarity of Decangi to Deceangli has biased the interpretation of the Roman conquest of the Marches. Scapula's campaign against the 'Deceangli' was for long assumed to have started from a legionary fortress at Wroxeter; but the legionary occupation there is now known to have begun no earlier than the 60s. The nearest legionary fortress of the 50's was probably at or near Wall in Staffordshire, separated from Clwyd by most of the Cornovian land.

According to Tacitus the Decangian campaign rendered quantities of loot so the tribe in question should be numerous, powerful and wealthy. The area of the Marches where field and excavation evidence

Fig 30 Roman military sites in Wales and the Marches

A Alcester	H Hindwell	TW Tedstone Wafer
B Bromfield	JL Jay Lane	TyM Tomen y Mur
BB Brampton Bryan	L Leintwardine	W Whittington
C Cound	LC Llanfair Caereinion	Wa Walltown
CA Craven Arms	LH Linley Hill	Wf Walford
Cd Caer-din	LM Little Mountain	Wi Wistanstow
Cl Clifton-on-Teme	M Monmouth	Wo Woolston
D Duncote	MC Mortimer's Cross	Wor Worcester
E Eaton Constantine	N Neath Y	Yarkhill
F Forden Gaer	R Rowton	
G Greensforge	S Sheet, Ludford	

points unequivocally to such a tribe is, with no possible rival, the Herefordshire basin. By comparison the few hillforts of Clwyd must represent a far smaller population even if they were still occupied in AD 48. Their poverty in finds is notorious and they have yet to be shown to have been occupied over long periods of time.

The equation of Decangi with Deceangli remains unproven but the fate of the Herefordshire hillforts fits better with that to be expected of the tribe that was the object of Scapula's campaign, surely a punitive one to show that Rome's enemies could expect no quarter. Most of the huts at Croft Ambrey and Midsummer Hill were burnt and the sites abandoned. Credenhill's huts were dismantled and the area given over to shallow pits dated to the early Roman period. The passage of Scapula's troops is the likely cause of this wrecking of communities that had been in place for over 400 years. It is not surprising that the area's record under the Romans is negligible, its only town, Kenchester, one of the smallest
in the province.

This reasoning would explain why Caratacus did not then raise his standard at Credenhill but chose the Silures instead. After bringing Legio XX to the west from Colchester, Scapula entered the territory of the Silures. He could hardly have done this safely unless he had already taken Herefordshire, thus enabling him to cross the northern Silurian frontier. This was probably from Clyro, for without a contest Caratacus left the Silures and moved north to the Ordovices. Retreat before battle would seem uncharacteristic of the man unless his position was irretrievably threatened either by the vacillation of the Silures themselves or by the threat of encirclement. As the Silures went on fighting until the 70s it is unlikely that they turned against Caratacus now. On the other hand a glance at the relief map of Wales reveals the control that would have been exercised by a Roman force in the Clyro-Brecon lowlands. The Usk valley to the west and the Wye to the north-west offered routes by which to outmanoeuvre British forces in South Wales.

From this reasoning it follows that Caratacus' retreat was well to the west and his final stand in 51 north of the Severn. This shifts the battle area away from the border hillforts on which earlier antiquaries imagined the final encounter; but no force large enough to oppose the Roman army would have trapped itself inside hillforts like the Herefordshire Beacon or Coxall Knoll. The case for Cefn Carnedd hillfort in the upper Severn valley, restated by St Joseph, must face the same objection. However, the area from here downstream to Newtown, which Webster has favoured, has the advantage of drawing the Romans into the Welsh massif, which Jones' recent advocacy of Llanymynech does not. This, again, is a hillfort even though an exceptionally large one, enclosing 54 hectares and standing 150 metres above the plain. There are crop marks of Roman military sites, including Llansantffraid-ym-Mechain stores depot, within a mile to the south-west and the position meets the Tacitean requirements of a fordable river and high crags opposite. With the Roman base south-west of the hill, Caratacus' subsequent flight to the Brigantes would seem feasible. The same would have been true of Newtown.

Legionary forces on campaign camped overnight in rectangular, single-ditched camps with rounded corners and gates towards the middle of the sides. Most were ploughed flat long ago but as more are revealed by crop marks it may be possible to conjecture the course of Scapula's battle group. His was but the first of numerous campaigns in the Marches so there will also be camps of Gallus in 52-57, Veranius in 57-58, Paulinus in 59-61 and possibly Frontinus in 74-75. There were later occasions too when Roman control was temporarily weakened and fresh campaigns had to be undertaken. When these historical considerations are set beside the unlikely loss of much equipment, coins or pottery during an overnight stay, it will be realized that dating such camps is problematic.

Six key areas have camps that might be Scapulan. The most southerly is Clyro where a camp of more than six hectares is set about the site of a later fort where the Wye enters Herefordshire. A second is near Leintwardine where the north-south Watling Street West crosses the Teme valley route to Wales, with camps of ten hectares at Walford and 25.6 at Brampton Bryan. At Brompton, near Montgomery, a fort site is accompanied by three overlapping camps; and we have already noted the complex near Llanymynech at the confluence of the Vyrnwy and Tanat. On the Severn plain west of the Wrekin there are camps at Eaton Constantine, Cound and Wroxeter. The sixth strategic location is Rhyn Park, east of Chirk, with a 17.5 hectare campaign base and a fort of six hectares or more. Large marching camps are also known at Whittington, Stretford Bridge and Bromfield.

Scapula's campaigns took the frontier westwards, the new sites of the 50s including the legionary fortress at Usk and the ten-hectare fort at Clyro which may have replaced an earlier fort at Clifford. A temporary legionary base camp of only five hectares occupied Brandon Hill south of Leintwardine where, by the 60s, a two-hectare auxiliary fort was built at Jay Lane. In the same general period a fort of the same size was built at Wroxeter. Others at Canon Frome, Hindwell, Kentchurch and Monmouth may belong to the same decade. These, like most Roman first-century forts, would have had earth ramparts revetted with turf and one or two ditches outside. Jay Lane had timber gate towers as well as interval and corner towers constructed with timber 220 millimetres square, set in post-holes 900 millimetres square. The uniformity of the post sockets reminds us that the stockpiling of timber was an important preliminary to the permanent extension of the province. The legionary buildings, with large granaries, at Brandon and Usk would have made great demands on the timber yards.

Meanwhile there was continued trouble in western Britain, led by the Silures. By the time of Boudicca's rebellion in the east in AD 60 the Marches were occupied and the army was operating deep into Wales, even to Anglesey. Frontinus finally vanquished the Silures in 74-75 and by 78 all the tribes had been subdued. Legio XIV, whose barracks lie deep below the later town baths at Wroxeter, was stationed there by 60 but was later withdrawn from Britain and replaced by Legio XX. Usk was abandoned in the later sixties and a new legionary fortress constructed at Caerleon in the mid 70s to be occupied by Legio II Augusta. About AD79 Legio II Adiutrix built a fortress at Chester and when Legio XX returned from its Scottish campaign in 86, the Wroxeter fortress was dismantled and the legion moved into Chester in place of Legion II Adiutrix which was withdrawn from Britain.

Caerleon and Chester each held a legion of about 5000 men and controlled the southern and northern coastal routes into Wales. Tidal water facilitated the receipt of stores for themselves and the network of auxiliary forts that spread from the edge of the Marches throughout Wales. New forts were built at Usk, Abergavenny, Pen y Gaer and Brecon; and Walltown remained occupied. Jay Lane was dismantled and a timber successor built at Buckton around AD 80. With a turf rampart and timber gate towers it was little larger than Jay Lane but gained a riverside position where a good water supply could be enjoyed and a bath-house constructed. Northwards the next fort of this period is Forden Gaer which may have replaced an earlier fort at Brompton.

In the Marches north of the Severn there is little sign of continued military activity. Apart from Chester and the works depot at Holt, only Whitchurch has proven military occupation after 80. Most of the territory of the Cornovii in Shropshire and the Deceangli in Clwyd was either co-operative or sparsely populated.

The Roman frontier AD 80-160

Highland Wales was to remain a source of problems; and the army's difficulties were increased by even greater problems in Scotland. Wales was sometimes depleted to reinforce the north, and the Marches came to act again as the backline of defence in the west. The forts along the Usk were maintained after AD 80 but the occupation of Usk and Pen y Gaer probably did not outlast the first century by many years. Only Abergavenny remained until the mid second-century between Caerleon and Brecon while in the Central Marches Buckton, Walltown and Forden Gaer were garrisoned into the second century.

The Chester fortress Deva - Celtic for 'goddess', name of the Dee- was set on the north bank where the Dee flowed round a low sandstone plateau (fig 31). This provided a dry, elevated, level site near the head of a sheltered estuary, well placed to service both North Wales and north-west England. The line of the east and north walls was re-used in the Middle Ages and parts can still be seen; but to the south and west the medieval defences were pushed out to the very bank of the river and the demolished Roman walls were covered by buildings. Although part of the Roman quay survives below the medieval wall the Roman river course is now filled. Despite many changes in fortune, the outline of the Roman street plan still shows through. Eastgate and Watergate Streets follow Deva's *via principalis*, the main street across the fortress in front of its headquarters. At right angles to them, Bridge Street perpetuates the *via praetoria* and Northgate Street the *via decumana*. Minor east-west Roman roads are followed by Commonhall Street and Princess Street.

The fortress was unusually large, enclosing 24.3 hectares compared with the normal twenty. Tombstones show that it was occupied, and presumably built, by Legio II Adiutrix, although by 90 Legio XX Valeria Victrix had taken over. Its first turf and timber defences and wooden barracks were put up in the late 70s. In Trajan's reign, probably soon after 102, the rampart was fronted with stone and new stone gate towers were built. The internal magnificence of second-century Deva is known from its stone barracks, granaries and workshops as well as the great headquarters building, *principia*, that measures at least 101 by 74 metres. An intra-mural bath building with a covered exercise hall occupied a space 80 metres square. Outside the walls was a parade ground and amphitheatre, the latter originally in wood but reconstructed in stone; it is open to visitors. Some of Deva's stone buildings were probably rebuilt at the end of the third century following depredation by northern invaders, and occupation continued at least until the disasters of 368-9.

Deva's suburbs, to the east, south and west of the fortress have been discussed by Mason, and include a bath-house and *mansio*, or guest-house. Extensive cemeteries lie along the road to the north and that to the south beyond the Dee. At Heronbridge, two kilometres to the south, was a settlement with workshops and stores along Watling Street. A works-depot on the Dee at Holt made pottery and tiles.

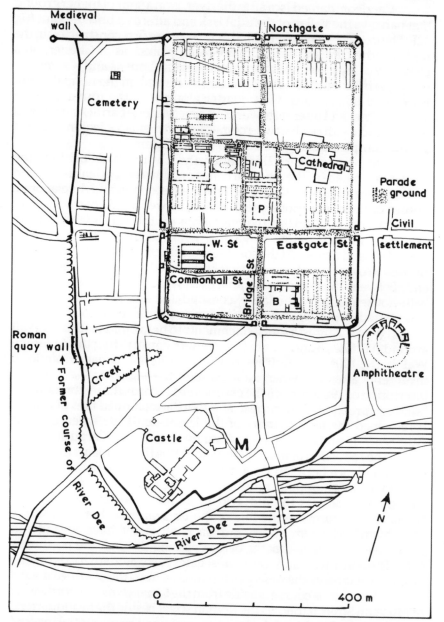

Fig 31 Chester fortress in relation to modern streets. Roman streets stippled.
B-baths G-granaries M-*mansio*   P-*principia*   W St-Watergate Street
(After Thompson 1959 and Petch 1969. Later detail in Mason 1986)

Caerleon, named Isca after the river, is on a spur of higher ground that narrows the valley of the tidal Usk and affords a bridge-point (fig 32). The defences, enclosing 20.5 hectares, were first constructed in the mid 70s, the clay and turf rampart being placed, as at Chester, on a corduroy of logs. Re-building in stone began about 87 and was mostly complete by about 100. The 1.7-metre stone wall in the rampart front is exposed in the north-west quarter along with the foundations of square corner and interval towers and several stone barracks, arranged in pairs, each with twelve two-roomed appartments for legionaries and a more complex unit against the road for officers.

The headquarters lies under the churchyard; behind, the *praetorium*, palace of the legate in command, has been identified. Also in this central area were the barracks of the first cohort and the elaborate houses of their centurions, *primi ordines*, as well as the barracks of an ordinary cohort. Next to the *praetorium* on the south-west was an exercise hall and a large magazine, while to the north-east was a workshop and stores. At the south-east end across the full width of the fortress a row of twenty-four barracks matched those at the north-west end. Between these and the *via principalis* was a hospital and a massive bath-house complex, the latter, consolidated and on public display, was started in the 70s and remained in use until about 230.

Legio II Augusta sent detachments to help build Hadrian's Wall around AD 122-28 and was in full strength constructing the Antonine Wall in the 140s. The fortress may have suffered damage from local insurgents after 196 when Albinus took the legion to Gaul, for an inscription of 198-209 from the churchyard records the restoration of a building, probably the *principia*, and there are stamped tiles of 213-22. It remained the headquarters of the legion until 293 when Legio II Augusta was probably taken to Gaul by the usurper Carausius.

The reduction of much of the site at this time explains the lack of correspondence between the fortress streets and the modern roads. There was more opportunity here than at Chester for post-Roman streets to cut across the old grid to avoid collapsed rubble. The Broadway conforms to the line of the *via principalis* but beyond the churchyard, Museum Street and Backhall Street have meandered south over the levelled baths before passing through the north-east gate. The north-west and south-west gates carry modern roads but the High Street crosses the defences ten metres from the south-east gate. Most of its sinuous course is aside from the *via praetoria* but north-west of Museum Street it follows the Roman street beside the headquarters, implying that this side of the building remained a substantial mass of masonry until a very late date.

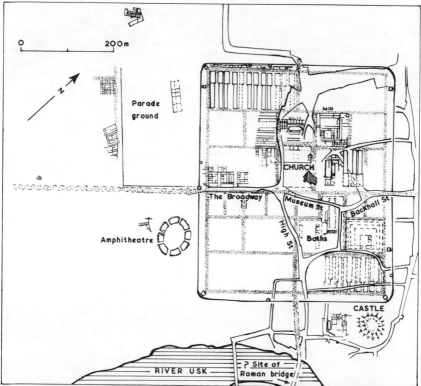

Fig 32 The Caerleon fortress in relation to the modern street plan. Roman roads are stippled. (After Boon 1962, 1972. Later detail in Zienciewicz 1990)

The amphitheatre stands outside the fortress, its oval arena measuring fifty-six by forty-two metres and the whole structure eighty-one by sixty-three metres. It could probably seat more than 6000, the nominal strength of a legion, and could have been used for combat-training as well as gladiatorial shows. Eight vaulted entrances permitted the rapid assembly or dispersal of even a capacity audience. It probably lay within the same walled annexe as the parade ground north of the Broadway and four bath buildings, including the large one under the medieval castle bailey. Outside the annexe was the *vicus*, a civil settlement traversed by the road from the south-west gate to wharves on the Usk. A building thirty metres square was possibly the *mansio*, an official guest-house; its construction in the mid second century may have marked state approval of the *vicus*, its houses, shops, warehouses, baths and, somewhere, temples of Diana and Mithras. The site at Bulmore, two kilometres upstream on the east bank, may

Plate 14   Buckton fort showing as a crop mark in ripening corn (W.A.Baker)

be another example like Heronbridge, of the detached depot that accompanies legionary fortresses on the Continent.

The late Flavian and Trajanic enthusiasm for reconstructing fortresses in stone was echoed in some of the auxiliary forts including Buckton (pl 14, fig 33). It enclosed 2.3 hectares and, like its timber predecessor and the earlier Jay Lane, probably housed a cavalry unit. The stone rampart wall was built in the early second century and provided with impressive gate towers flanking twin portals (fig 34). The overall dimensions of the east gate were 22.3 by 6.1 metres, this unusually large size allowing internal stone staircases, an amenity sometimes given to legionary gate towers but rare in auxiliary forts. Some buildings, including the granaries and headquarters, had stone foundations but most were still of timber.

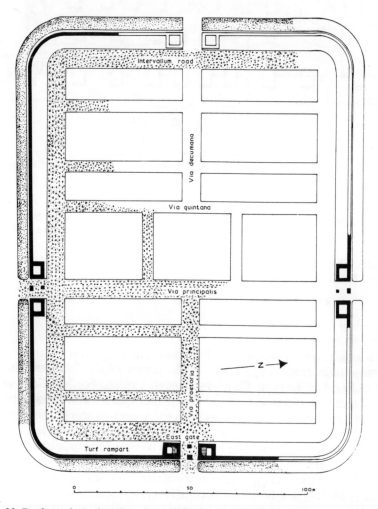

Fig 33 Buckton fort, showing stone defences and roads shaded where revealed
by aerial photographs or excavation (After Stanford 1968b, fig 10)

By about 140, with a general reduction of garrisons in the west,
Buckton was dismantled, the stonework being removed to ground
level. Similar sandstone, re-used, occurred in primary contexts in the
bath-house of AD 160 plus at Leintwardine. It probably came from
Buckton since such stone is absent to the east of the Clun.   There
must be other forts between Buckton and Forden Gaer ; and also
between Buckton and Walltown, an almost square fort covering 1.9

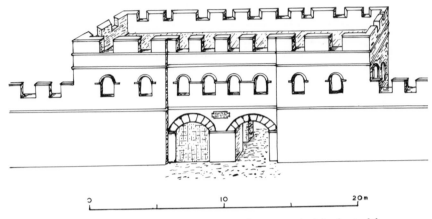

Fig 34 Reconstruction of Buckton's east gate *(porta praetoria)* adapted from
Richmond and Child's reconstruction of Housesteads west gate (1942)

hectare. The first-century rampart there was of turf with timber lacing;
a stone front was added after about 120.

The Roman frontier after 160

There was a further reduction of garrisons in Wales after 140 but the
Romans maintained large bases in the centre of the frontier with a
quadrilateral of forts at Caersws, Castell Collen, Forden Gaer and
Leintwardine about twenty-eight kilometres apart. All were occupied
in the second and third centuries with some occupation in the fourth.

The two sites in the Marches, Leintwardine and Forden Gaer,
share common features, seen by some to be more appropriate to civil
sites. Leintwardine village fort (fig 35) dates after 160, perhaps as late
as the 170s. It is on rising ground north of the Teme with a small annexe
holding a bath-house between fort and river. Its location along Watling
Street West seems previously to have been a civil settlement serving in
turn the garrisons of Jay Lane and Buckton as well as travellers on this
frontier road between Chester and Caerleon.

The character of any internal buildings, other than the bath-
house, is uncertain for the site is deeply eroded except in the lee of the
rampart, best seen along the north and west sides; the church stands
just inside the rampart on the east side. Measuring 4.5 hectares over the
rampart the main enclosure is about twice as large as Buckton. The
bath-house is more fitting for a a single cohort of 500 men, so the extra
space may have been used as a depot to supply other forts.

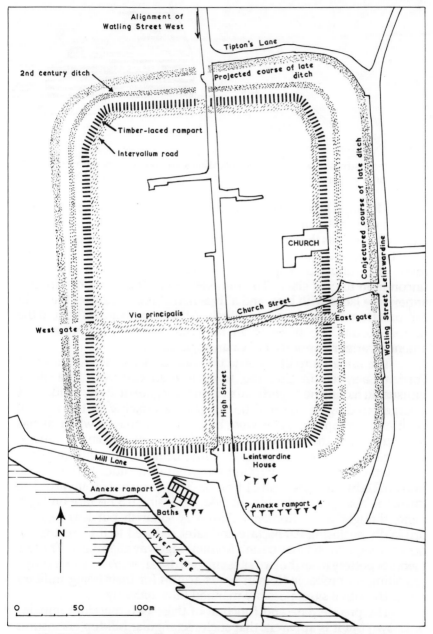

Fig 35 Leintwardine village fort showing defences and projected plan
of the main roads (After Stanford 1968b, amended)

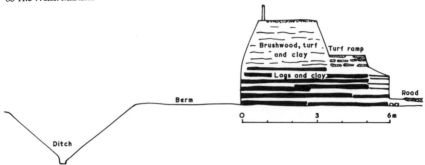

Fig 36 Reconstructed section of Leintwardine's second-century defences based on a section close to the north-west angle (After Stanford 1968b)

Although Leintwardine is unusually large for an auxiliary fort there is no convincing evidence of a specifically civilian occupation after 160, whereas the defences are indicative of military construction. They have a rectangular plan, with four gates positioned as in standard forts. The unusual shaping of all four angles gives a symmetry uncommon to civil sites. The unrevetted clay ramparts of fort and annexe are laced with logs, and a five-metre berm separates the main rampart from its accompanying ditch. All four excavations behind the rampart found the stone of an intervallum road, its course now amended after re-appraisal of Chantreyland section 3.

The same rampart construction and dimensions were used at Forden Gaer, rebuilt after 160, to enclose 3.1 hectares. The site is unusual in having no superficial evidence for gates in its long sides but a large building in the middle suggests a *principia* in the normal position. Perhaps the gates were blocked later, maybe when, as has been suggested, the road was taken straight through from the north to south gate, also a feature of the eventual Leintwardine village plan.

Other sites that may reflect recurrent difficulties in the central hills are Tedstone Wafer and Clifton-on-Teme, north of Bromyard. The former is oblong and double-ditched, enclosing 0.5 hectare on High Lane, thought to be Roman. Clifton is squarish but less regular, originally enclosing 0.6 hectare and later reduced to 0.4 hectare; the nearby modern road may be on a Roman ridgeway alignment. The few pieces of pottery from the two sites suggest use after 150 and their ridge-top siting on probable Roman roads argues for their being military rather than civil sites, possibly manned intermittently.

The precise date and function of these two therefore remains unknown but it is apparent that such rectangular hill-top enclosures are not uncommon in the Marches. North of Clyro, Little Mountain Camp encloses 0.2 hectare and is approached by a road that Rennell traced branching off the presumed Mortimer's Cross - Clyro road. The earthwork of a similar camp survives on Linley Hill, near Bishop's Castle. Baker has photographed comparable sites as crop-marks at Rowton and Woolston near Craven Arms and the writer has seen others from the air at Sheet near Ludlow and at Yarkhill.

In summary, the military history of the Marches falls into three periods. From 48 till 74 the Romans, having gained control of Herefordshire and north Gwent, extended their rule to the whole of the Marches. In the second period, following the establishment of Caerleon and Chester, and the establishment of forts all over Wales, several forts in the Marches were abandoned while others were maintained, notably along the Usk and in the central hills. Finally, from about 160 a new policy saw the reconstruction of large forts at Leintwardine and Forden Gaer, in the central Marches between the two fortresses. Like Chester these remained in use until the late fourth century, whereas Caerleon was evacuated by the end of the third. The threat to the Roman province had shifted. Instead of the Silures being the persistent enemies, northern barbarians were now ready to move in should Rome's hold relax.

Civilian developments (fig 37)

The exploitation of the Marches by the new rulers was modified by the military necessity of keeping erstwhile enemies divided and weak. The Roman period saw a striking reduction of large settlements of hillfort size with little evidence of lesser nucleations replacing them.

In the northern part of the border there have been excavations in the interiors of nine out of about thirty hillforts - Eddisbury, Maiden Castle, Moel y Gaer, Old Oswestry, the Berth, the Breidden, Oliver's Point, Ebury and the Wrekin. Only at the Berth, the Breidden and Oliver's Point has Roman pottery been found; there is little doubt that the others were not occupied as villages during the Roman period. In the Severn valley the Romans may have been content to remove the natives from their most strongly entrenched or naturally fortified sites like Old Oswestry and the Wrekin, allowing occupation to continue in more vulnerable lowland hillforts. The second part of this hypothesis leans heavily on the evidence from Oliver's Point, and until a weakly defended hillfort in the plains is extensively excavated an alternative explanation should be kept in mind - that all the hillforts of the northern border were evacuated at or before the Roman conquest.

Fig 37 The Roman Marches - Civil sites and the legionary fortresses.
All major sites are shown and any others in the text.
List of deserted hillforts:

1 Moel y Gaer, Rhosesmor	2 Eddisbury	3 Maiden Castle, Bickerton
4 Old Oswestry	5 Ebury	6 The Wrekin
7 Ffridd Faldwyn	8 The Roveries	9 Titterstone Clee
10 Caynham	11 Croft Ambrey	12 Credenhill
13 Midsummer Hill	14 Twyn y Gaer,	15 Coed y Bwnydd
16 Llanmelin Wood	Cwmyoy	

Sites shown by initials: Ca Caldicott   Cr Cruckton   G Goldcliff
M Magor   R Redwick   W Whitley   WV Whitchurch Vagas

The desolation of the hillforts marked the end of a distinct settlement period when the hillfort dominated its environs and the communities were large and closely knit within their defences. Life along these lines had demanded a complex code of behaviour, with acceptance of duties that supported the community through the stress of raids and more serious conflict. It may be that the hillfort experiment had died a natural death in the extreme north of the Marches before the Romans arrived; and without them that part of the border would have fallen readily before the Roman army, even as the non-hillfort south-east did in 43. Although a hillfort itself could not be held for long against Roman siege tactics, a zone of such fortifications gave time for the organization of defence in depth and facilitated communications and prompt response. The Romans had to destroy this unifying social and political influence by dispersing the population, reducing once proud strongholds to deserted villages. Those leaders who were not seduced to the Roman dominion and yet were spared to continue farming did so in fragmented communities, shorn of authority first by defeat and then by isolation. At least that seems a likely interpretation of the following evidence.

In the Severn valley, where the single- and double-ditched enclosures are not correlated with hillfort chronologies, it is possible that some hillforts were already breaking up before the conquest; although Old Oswestry, the Breidden and possibly the Wrekin were not yet quite empty. If the Shropshire and nearby Powys sites overlooking the Severn had been as closely occupied as their Herefordshire counterparts there should have been some 12,000 people in the area. Some of these are to be located in those ditched enclosures like the one at Sharpstone Hill enclosing 0.1 hectare (p 48) that continued from an Iron Age beginning into the second century AD. The majority, however, must have been in open settlements about which we have little idea. If they were isolated farmsteads like Sharpstone Hill and Bromfield there could be around 1,200 to be identified in the Severn valley alone.

It is clear that the Roman conquest saw the final disruption of the hillfort nucleations and the almost universal substitution of small units. Most of these would have been carved out of the fields around the hillforts but there would have been new intake too, especially around Wroxeter. The new city market and sense of security may have attracted folk from the hills who left behind neglected sheep pastures. Perhaps these Cornovian farms included newcomers from the hillforts of the central Marches where there is no evidence of Romano-British occupation despite excavations on Burrow Camp, Caynham, Croft Ambrey, Ffridd Faldwyn, the Roveries and Titterstone Clee.

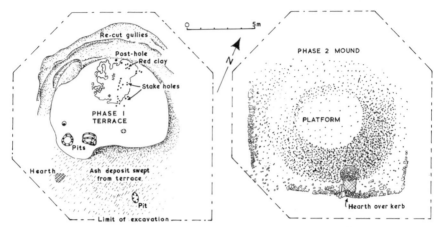

Fig 38 The successive forms of the Croft Ambrey Romano-British sanctuary
(Based on Stanford 1974a, figs 64 and 65)

Only at Croft Ambrey have even a few Romano-British sherds been found within the main enclosure, the village occupation of which terminated with the conquest. Nevertheless, the old inhabitants continued to worship in front of their old rampart, for within the bivallate defences of the hillfort annexe they prepared a terrace for ceremonies involving animal sacrifices probably supported on stakes (fig 38). The red clay floor of the terrace was kept clean, the debris from these ceremonies being swept down the slope below. It consisted of charcoal, numerous sherds of Romano-British pottery, burnt bones of sheep, pig and cattle, and several bronze brooches. The use of this terrace sanctuary lasted from the first to at least the mid second century. It was then covered by a flat-topped mound nearly twelve metres square at the base and a metre high. A rough drystone kerb with rounded corners survived on three sides - enough alone to deny a recent suggestion that it was a rabbit warren.

The annexe defences nearest the sanctuary had been breached in Roman times as though to give more direct access to the shrine from the hillside below where some of the displaced inhabitants may have been resettled. Others may have moved north-west, where Baker has photographed five Cornovian-type enclosures within five kilometres of Leintwardine. Many who survived the fire and pillage of Scapula's campaign would have been taken as slaves and transported to distant road-works. Here, as in the Shropshire hills, the landscape changed. Valleyward fields may have replaced the former rough grazing and glade pastures; the upland farms reverted to scrub and soon forest.

Further south a more selective policy is indicated. The huts of Midsummer Hill, like those of Croft Ambrey, were burnt and no village re-established. By contrast there was long continued occupation of Sutton Walls and Poston Camp; and Roman sherds have come from Dinedor, Aconbury, Wall Hills Ledbury and Uphampton Camps. It looks as though some natives stayed on in most of the hillforts of middle, lowland Herefordshire; but not in all. The few Romano-British finds over the dismantled Credenhill huts need be no later than the 60s. By then, if not before, the policy of evacuation probably extended to all the more powerfully placed hillforts, like Credenhill, Chase Wood, Little Doward, Symonds Yat and Capler Camp.

One way and another, something like half the hillfort population of Herefordshire was probably displaced - about 13,000 people. If all were resettled in single farmsteads there will be more than a thousand such to locate. By making the most generous allowance for settlement on known Romano-British town and villa sites in the county, the total of displaced persons might be reduced to around 8,000. At present we have but a shadowy impression of perhaps a score of possible farmsteads.

The abandonment of hillforts probably extended southwards to the Severn estuary. Twyn y Gaer, our viewpoint on the Black Mountains, was abandoned; and no Roman pottery or structure was found in Coed y Bwnydd, much lower at 198 metres. Along the southern edge of the Marches, free from the tangle of hills and narrow valleys, the treatment of hillforts varied. East of the Wye, the hillfort in Lydney Park was probably abandoned at the conquest; but in the second century iron ore mining brought renewed activity until the fourth century when an imposing temple was built and dedicated to Nodens, probably a Celtic god who combined concern for healing, hunting and the sea (fig 39). It represents a massive investment in the profitable field of piety, equipped to cater for pilgrims from a wide area. The centre of a healing cult, it had a long cubicled building, the *abaton*, in which invalids might rest assured of being visited in their sleep by the benevolent Nodens. For their further comfort there was a large courtyard-plan guest-house and suite of baths.

First-century samian ware at Llanmelin Wood Camp implies some activity there for a while, and late third- and fourth-century pottery echoes the later revival of interest seen in some hillforts elsewhere. Abundant first-century material from Sudbrook Camp has led to the idea that it was taken over as a supply port prior to the establishment of Caerleon. Its continuance as a ferry terminal would explain the less intensive evidence for the rest of the Roman period.

With the exception of Sudbrook, the larger hillforts of Gwent were probably abandoned and the population dispersed. The Romano-British sherds from the small univallate Bryngwyn Camp indicate activity within or nearby but there is little else to go on. Roman material from buried sites along the coastal plain at Uskmouth, Goldcliff, Redwick and Magor reflect dispersal and offshore Roman drainage channels confirm land reclamation and subsequent inundation, the latter about the end of the second century. Another movement of population would thus have ensued within 150 years of the conquest.

The Romanized Britons

The Roman occupation brought important changes for the surviving self-sufficient farmers. The tribute demanded more corn to feed the hungry garrisons in Wales, so there may have been an increase in arable. Some technological improvements also probably permeated the rural communities. Rotary querns now became general throughout the border, and at some time stone malt-ovens, formerly thought to be corn-driers, were introduced - at Sutton Walls for example. The rustic VCP salt-containers soon disappeared; and the old pottery firms turned to large-scale production of wheel-turned vessels.

There were of course the more romanized elements of settlement and industry in the Marches - the towns, villas, potteries and mines, linked by a road system that was quite new in style and concept. The straight metalled roads possibly coincided in places with prehistoric routes but Watkins' theory of an extensive pre-Roman system of straight tracks lacks proof.

The new Roman roads (fig 30) were not designed to serve the native communities but to communicate with the forts. Military needs required a north-south road from Chester to Caerleon which connected Whitchurch, Wroxeter, Leintwardine, Kenchester, Abergavenny and Usk. North of Hereford an eastern route branched off this to cross the Wye at Hereford and proceed south to Monmouth and Caerwent. Feeders to the Welsh forts ran from Chester to North Wales and the Upper Dee valley; from Wroxeter to Forden Gaer and the Upper Severn; from Leintwardine along the Teme valley towards Castell Collen; from Kenchester westwards along the Wye valley; from Abergavenny west along the Usk valley; and from Caerleon via the Vale of Glamorgan to Neath and Carmarthen. Two main routes entered the Marches from the east: in the north, from Penkridge to Wroxeter and to Chester; in the south from Gloucester north-west to Hereford and south-west to Caerleon. Between these Canon Frome must have been linked with Worcester; and another road from Greensforge followed

Corve Dale to Craven Arms and thence to Forden Gaer.

Three walled towns grew up in the Marches, at Wroxeter, Kenchester and Caerwent - one for each of the main tribes, the Cornovii, Decangi and Silures. They differ greatly in form and history, and between them show many of the diverse facets of Romano-British towns, the creation of which was an important part of imperial policy. The town was a centre of government for the administration of justice and taxation. It held the houses and shops of immigrant merchants and other professionals who expected the usual Roman amenities of streets and water-supply - and the promise, at least, of temples and baths. The town's purpose was also to wean the more ambitious and co-operative natives from their traditional way of life and graft them on the imperial system.

Wroxeter, Viroconium Cornoviorum, became the capital of the Cornovii but started as a legionary fortress (fig 40). When this was demolished about AD 90 its bath-house, below the later forum, was still unfinished. It was west of, and so outside, the fortress rampart excavated by Webster beneath the later town's market-house, just east of Watling Street. Wilson's new detailed plan of the town added confirmatory evidence to Webster's conclusion that the Watling Street rampart, the 'early ditch' of previous descriptions, and the later line of the eastern city wall, define the west, north and east sides of the

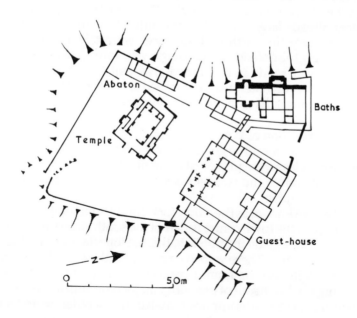

Fig 39 The Lydney Park temple complex (After Lewis 1966 fig 119)

fortress; an intervallum road and signs of rampart buildings put the fourth close to the line of a modern road. The area, measured over the anticipated rampart front, would be about 20 hectares, close to the size of Caerleon. It appears that although the north and south extremities of the presumed *via principalis* were re-used for the town plan, most of the later streets were on a different grid.

The measurement of 380 metres over the two exterior north-south roads almost matches the distance over the longitudinal intervallum roads of Caerleon and Chester. From this starting point it can be seen that the Wroxeter town street plan is in fact very close to that of the Chester fortress. It looks as though a detachment from that garrison was given the job of laying out the new town, and used the measurements already in their log books. By then the fortress defences had been levelled on at least three sides. This history helps explain the enigma of Wroxeter: fourth largest town in the province, although far away in the north-west. There was already the site of a legionary fortress of twenty hectares and nine hectares of extramural buildings between Watling Street and the Severn. Use of the Chester grid, transverse to the original fortress lay-out, would have added seven hectares; so the new town started with at least thirty-six hectares of developable land.

When the first-century town was fortified the defences would have enclosed the corners of the grid and any ribbon development along the roads to north and south. The larger circuit held fifty-two hectares, already large enough to rank fifth in Roman Britain. In the late second century the earthwork defences were taken across the Bell Brook to bring the defended area to eighty hectares. There are few signs of buildings or roads in the added area which perhaps anticipated growth that never materialized or served another purpose. Richmond suggested it might have taken in a sacred area; and Wacher that it was farmland.

The extension of Wroxeter beyond its military legacy may have resulted, as Richmond argued, from the immigration of the native landowning class in search of city amenities and security; but only a dozen large houses and two temples are known from excavation and aerial photographs.

The wall known as the 'Old Work' (pl 15) which still towers eight metres high in the town centre is part of the south wall of an enormous exercise hall alongside the public baths, the foundations of which date from later than 160. There were cold plunge baths as well as warm and hot rooms with dry or humid conditions. A magnificent covered swimming pool went out of use with a major reorganization about 210. The late date of the baths implies a small initial population; indeed, the

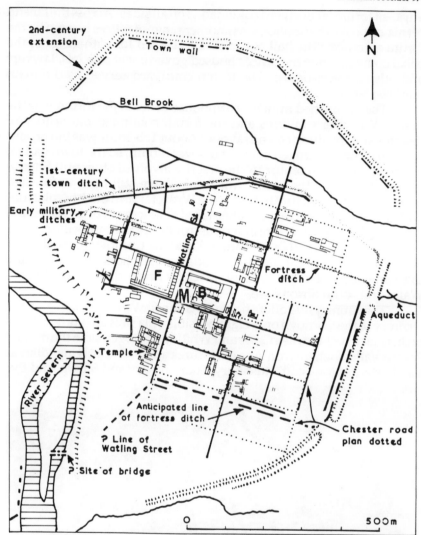

Fig 40 Wroxeter's plan with that of the Chester fortress roads superimposed. (Wroxeter details, mostly from aerial photographs, taken from Baker 1968, 1970. Later detail in Wilson 1984) F forum; B baths; M *macellum*

forum and basilica, dedicated to Hadrian, was not completed until 130. It was bigger than Silchester's, measuring eighty-one by one hundred and twenty-one metres, and shows the town to be relatively wealthy, or ambitious. The basilica was a long aisled hall flanked by offices; the adjacent forum, a courtyard colonnaded on all sides. Across the far end of this, opposite the basilica, was another range of offices pierced by the forum entrance. The hall of the basilica served for gatherings of the tribal council, while the offices housed government officials, lawyers and other professionals. The forum courtyard served as the main market-place.

The unfinished military bath-house beneath the forum was the first of Wroxeter's failures and the forum continued the history of disaster and misdirected endeavour. About 165-185 it was burnt, and a century later destroyed again and never rebuilt, so the town had no forum in the fourth century. The first fire involved other buildings to the south but not the baths, which may have still been unfinished without a superstructure to burn. The Wroxeter fire roughly coincides with the construction of the timber-laced defences of Forden Gaer and Leintwardine, and may hint at serious trouble, perhaps rebellion, in the Welsh border in the 160s. Richmond saw the Cornovian privilege of having their militia enrolled as a regular unit, Cohors I Cornoviorum, to be an encouragement to resist attack by brigands from the hills of Wales and south Shropshire.

The countryside offers no explanation for Wroxeter's size. In the territory of the Cornovii only eight possible villa sites are known; three of them, at Cruckton, Lea Cross and Whitley, are together in the middle Severn valley, where Iron Age enclosures abound. Outlying villas at Yarchester, Acton Scott, Rushbury, Stanton Lacy and Stowe, and the

Plate 15   Wroxeter baths, the Old Work

establishment at Linley, do little to alter the impression of poverty that surrounds everything but the capital of the Cornovii.

The western edge of the territory lay along the metalliferous zone of the Shelve district and Linley may have been the headquarters for processing lead. Mining started at least as early as Hadrian's reign, as inscriptions of 'IMP HADRIANI AUG' on five lead pigs from around Minsterley testify, but the enterprise was short-lived. This may have been due to the absence of a rich silver content, or to the decline in demand once Wroxeter's needs for conduits and baths had been met. Copper was probably won from veins around Habberley and was taken in larger quantities from mines on Llanymynech Hill. The Deceanglian lead mines on Halkyn Mountain started as early as 74 with much of the metal being shipped via the Mersey or Dee.

If the Iron Age capital had been, like Wroxeter, in the Severn valley, it is more likely to have been at Bury Walls, enclosing eight hectares, where Camden wrote of Roman bricks and coins being found, than at the Wrekin. However, the dispersal of hillfort communities may have been accompanied by a change of capital too, perhaps from Titterstone Clee's twenty-eight hectares or Llanymynech's fifty-six.

The Wye basin

In the lands to the south, conjecturally occupied by the Decangi, the price exacted for the tribe's earlier assault on the infant Roman province was heavy indeed. Its only walled settlement is the roadside agglomeration at Kenchester, Magnis (fig 41). It has been argued that a fort preceded the town but no structural evidence is yet to hand to demonstrate this. The timber nucleus may have been at the junction of the Watling Street West with the Clyro road but most of the lateral development took place to the west, the junction being left outside the kite-shaped enclosure of the town wall. Inside were several large houses but aerial photographs suggest large areas without stone buildings. Beneath the excavated buildings was a layer of charcoal, the debris of burnt buildings. The disaster might be related to the Sutton Walls hillfort massacre which left at least twenty-four corpses in a shallow grave outside the west gate, six decapitated; but neither event is reliably dated.

The rebuilding may have introduced a change of alignments. The axial road is east-west with north-south branches, presumably primary. An angle of 105⁰ to it is used by some roads and most of the stone buildings away from the main street. This would seem to make the alignment secondary despite the attraction of its parallelism with

Plate 16   Kenchester bastion foundations on the west wall of the town

the Watling Street West which Wilmott used to support a primary construction. One large building is at an angle of 50° to the main street. With so many alignments it is probable that most roads were laid to serve a building or two, not an *insula*, let alone a town. The lateral development of Magnis was small but it was embanked in the second century and a stone wall was inserted later. Bastions were added, probably in the late fourth century (pl 16) when, too, a west gate portal was blocked.

Wacher listed Magnis as a village, one of only six bastioned villages, four of them grouped in eastern England, plus Mildenhall, Wiltshire. Such provision suggests some administrative functions; but there are no inscriptions, literary references or buildings to back securely its geographical appropriateness as capital of the Decangi. It is usually assumed, on the basis of the milestone bearing RPCD (p 75) to have been administered from Cirencester; but if the Decangi still enjoyed a separate existence Kenchester must have been their capital. Its walled area of nine hectares is remarkably small but Caister-by-Norwich, the Icenian capital, held only fourteen and Moridunum, thought to be capital of the Demetae, only six.

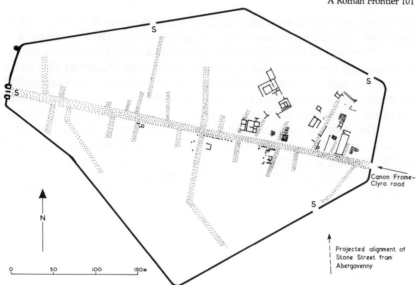

Fig 41 Kenchester: excavated west gate and bastion (Heys and Thomas 1962) internal foundations (Jack and Hayter 1926) and roads on aerial photographs (Baker 1966). S - Gates on Stukeley's map 1721.

Magnis could only have taken a few of the four thousand tribesmen evicted from nearby Credenhill Camp; others must have been resettled on farms around the town. The stone buildings of one just east of the town, formerly thought to be a temple, were shown by Wilmott and Rahtz to overlie the ditches and post-holes of an Iron Age farm, but without evidence of continuity. A mosaic pavement at Bishopstone and a villa at New Weir are other signs of development in the vicinity. Another favoured agricultural area was probably in the lower Frome valley, west of the settlement of Epocessa at Canon Frome. The nucleus of this settlement, west of the early fort, probably originated as a posting station at the junction of the east-west Kenchester road with the north-south one from Gloucester but spread along the latter towards Stretton Grandison.

Herefordshire's other named settlement, Ariconium, is a problem. Building debris and pottery is widespread around Bury Hill, east of Ross-on-Wye but no defences and only one building are recorded. This open settlement, close to iron ore in the Forest of Dean, was devoted to industry requiring ample space for work and waste disposal. There is much slag north of the Bromsash road where Bridgewater found primitive furnaces and working hollows. The place was included in the Antonine Itinerary, a second-century road-book, and the name survived, as Erging or Archenfield, for the post-Roman district west of the Wye. Another iron-working site was excavated at Whitchurch.

The villa of Huntsham was sighted from the air within a splendid loop of the Wye. Its excavated buildings included the main corridor-house, a minor dwelling and an aisled barn, the house being protected by a thick precinct wall. The site covers in all about eight hectares and was in use from the second century until the late fourth.

The surface finds within the Herefordshire basin are few but show a bias in favour of well-drained soils on gravel in the valleys of the Wye, Lugg and Frome. There were also probably village communities in hillforts like Sutton Walls, Poston and Uphampton Camp; but overall there was probably something of an agricultural retreat from the margins due to depopulation in the wake of the conquest.

The Dean-Trelleck uplands

The territory between the Decangi and the Silures was but thinly populated. Roads linked the nodal settlements around the early forts at Abergavenny (Gobannium), Usk (Burrio) and Monmouth (Blestium) but their extent and status is unknown. Blestium had an interest in iron-working and Gobannium, named after 'the river of blacksmiths', exploited blackband ore from the Coal Measures. An iron furnace was also found in post-military levels at Burrio. High grade haematite from the Crease limestone in the Forest of Dean was especially prized for primitive working and although most ore would have been won by quarrying, there was also mining, as demonstrated by the shallow shaft and gallery inside Lydney hillfort. The forests would have been extensively felled for charcoal but probably recovered as coppice.

Lydney Park's location on the forest edge above the estuary must have been especially attractive to those who had earned their wealth in the towns but the improvement of the enclosing hillfort rampart against brigands in the fourth century, rather than later, was an understandable precaution for the safety of priests and guests.

Across southern Gwent several Roman locations are known and many more must be covered by silt. Pottery kilns at Caldicot are just north of a presumed villa site; and Romano-British material has come from Magor and Goldcliff, and from a settlement at Chepstow. A temple at Gwehelog near Usk has been photographed from the air. The port functions of the extramural settlement at Caerleon may have enabled it to prosper even after the withdrawal of the legion.

More than three quarters of Silurian territory lay west of the Usk and under military control well into the second century. It is not surprising therefore that their only town and capital, Caerwent (Venta Silurum), should be behind the front, close to the tribe's eastern boundary. There is no evidence of a pre-Roman capital in the vicinity. Llanmelin Wood Camp, only two kilometres away, recalls the spatial relationship of Credenhill and Kenchester, but the Gwent fort only encloses two hectares. Caerwent may have succeeded to Sudbrook Camp (p 72) less than five kilometres to the south-east. As a port it was well placed to maintain contact with the far-flung Silurian lands along the northern shore of the Severn. The Iron Age capital may however have been further west in the Vale of Glamorgan.

This argument is in harmony with the view that Caerwent developed ribbon-wise along the Caerleon road before the second-century reduction of tension in South Wales made a western Silurian capital feasible. An alternative hypothesis is that the town was on the site of an earlier fort to which the first-century pottery belongs. The rectangular layout of the eighteen-hectare town may date to the third century; and the similarity of its plan with that of the Icenian capital may reflect the poverty and lack of spontaneous development of two tribes hammered by Rome for hostility and rebellion.

About three-fifths of Caerwent's building have been planned and show it to possess most characteristics of Romano-British towns. The main street, here the Gloucester-Caerleon road, traverses the town from east to west gates. Beside it, in the centre, was the forum and basilica, the Corinthian capitals of which indicate construction by about 150. Covering eighty by fifty-six metres, it dominated the town but was small by comparison with its British contemporaries, being less than half the size of Wroxeter's forum. In all, the public buildings take up a quarter of the excavated area, including a bath-house south of the forum and a fourth-century temple to the east. The latter was of a common Romano-Celtic plan with a central cella six metres square, surrounded by an ambulatory two metres wide, the whole precinct, thirty-four by twenty metres, enclosed within its own boundary wall. Just outside the town's east wall was a temple with an octagonal cella central to a circular temenos forty metres diameter.

A large building just inside the south gate is thought to be a *mansio*, with twenty rooms around three sides of a courtyard, the fourth being the town wall. An elliptical structure with diameters of forty-four and thirty-seven metres lies north of the forum, and might be an amphitheatre or cattle market. Caerwent contains more than its share of large courtyard houses, upwards of thirty metres square. They were splendidly furnished, some with mosaic floors, in a style to suit the curial class recruited from the tribal aristocracy. They enjoyed piped water and at least one had a bath suite.

Such houses represent in unequivocal terms the estrangement of the tribal leaders from the communities with whom their forebears had shared common danger and toil; but their stone construction at least could be a late development. The early fourth-century house in Pound Lane, for example, was the first courtyard building to be erected on that site. In their final form, with gardens and orchards, these houses and the offices and amenities of the state and its ruling class took up nearly all Venta Silurum. Within the excavated areas some twenty narrow oblong buildings, mostly end-on to the main street, were probably occupied by shopkeepers and craftsmen.

If Caerwent started life without defences it may have reflected confidence that the army would quickly subdue the natives and peaceful commercial development would promptly follow. The eventual need to fortify this and other towns marks, in part, a failure of this programme. An earth rampart was built around Caerwent some time after 130, following the removal of most of the auxiliary troops from South Wales. Local brigands, finding cover in the wooded valleys to the north, may then have threatened the safety of the town. In the second half of the third century a massive stone wall was inserted in the rampart front, three metres wide and still five metres high in places. Four gates pierced it, one towards the middle of each side; the single-portal North Gate has been restored.

At a late date Venta Silurum was also provided with bastions, the north-west one dated not earlier than 350. They are upstanding, or recorded, fifty metres apart along only the south and north walls and demonstrate new tactics against enemies who were to be numbered in hundreds rather than tens before the end of the fourth century. They could have carried large catapults to disperse such hordes.

Whenever they were in sufficient strength the brigands from the hills and raiders from the sea would have sought the special prizes that lay in the towns, which were virtually the only repositories for the civil wealth of the Marches. Such wealth may partly reflect their own late commercial success but is more likely to have been the concentration of what small surplus was produced over a wide area around. Later on, when raiders in larger numbers sought land as well as loot, the attacks on towns would have had the military objective of knocking out the local militia. The origins and influence of the new terrorists are better considered in the next chapter, for by the late fourth century Rome's interest in Britain was waning. Casey has shown that coins prove a military presence in Wales for a decade after Magnus Maximus took the legions to Gaul in 383 but it was slight.

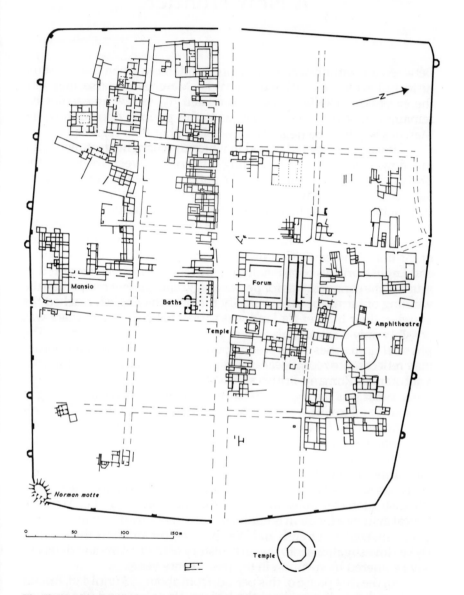

Fig 42 Plan of Caerwent, somewhat simplified from plans by V.E.Nash-
Williams (1930 and 1968); north-east bastions added from D.o.E.
handbook 1976 (Crown Copyright - reproduced with permission of the
controller of Her Majesty's Stationery Office)

CHAPTER EIGHT

A New Frontier

Between the withdrawal of the legions and the Norman Conquest the historical evidence relating to the Welsh Marches is sparse; and with the exception of Offa's Dyke and related dykes few archaeological remains can be confidently ascribed to this period. Accordingly, the Marches will here be treated as a whole, rather than regionally.

It was a protracted period in which the changing fortunes of the invading English, and the shifting alliances between them and the British kingdoms, culminated in the political supremacy of the Anglo-Saxons in what is now England and the sharper definition of Celtic culture in what came to be Wales. Some of the questions to be asked are quite basic: To what extent was the British population replaced by the English? And did refugees swarm westwards from the battlefields of the north and east? Certainly the facility with which British kings and English princes occasionally allied in common cause suggests that much of the conquest was for personal aggrandisement rather than the winning of farms for followers. By the time the English reached the Marches their hunger for land was somewhat abated and there was possibly only a small replacement of population in many areas. The physical similarities of the present population either side of the border may reflect more recent peaceful migrations but may also result from a substantial Romano-British survival.

What was the legacy left by the Romans? As well as looking at the roads and towns we must consider the negative effects of Rome's rule and see how far the neglect of certain areas influenced later events. In Gwent, large post-Roman estates may be successors to villa estates but their settlements are archaeologically elusive. Earlier ideas about the influence of Celtic saints based on church dedications and medieval texts have been largely discounted, their reported lives seen to be late distortions for political and ecclesiastical propaganda. Archaeological evidence for them is minimal. Later there are the frontier works built between the English and Welsh, foremost amongst them Offa's Dyke. Investigations into the early history of town plans and defences have gathered momentum in the past twenty years.

In the first phase of this period, from about 393 until 430, Britain was learning to live without the legions. In the second, the English came in large numbers and by the early seventh century had annexed the English lowlands. The third phase saw the Marches taken over and Offa's Dyke built about 784; the fourth phase ends in 1066.

While ruled by Rome, Britain had relied on professional soldiers for its defence; indeed, in the later Empire it was illegal for citizens to wear arms. When the legions left in about 393 they were expected to come back. There were, after all, still some troops in the north and possibly some in the central Marches. When the bulk of these left for the Continent with Constantine III in 407 they were not to return. In these circumstances senior citizens may have acquired control of local town garrisons who would have been attentive to anyone willing to pay them now that Imperial interest had faded and little coinage was coming into the country.

Disgust with Rome's failure to provide for the defence of the province led the Britons to take over the government. This would have been no later than 410 when, in response to their plea for military support against the Picts, they were told by the emperor Honorius to look to their own defence. The construction of town bastions is generally thought to be later than the Anglo-Saxon and Pictish raids of 367 although their variety of form and irregular spacing may denote construction over a long period, the outcome of local rather than imperial decree. Kenchester and Caerwent have similarly disposed bastions of pentagonal outline, contrasting with Cirencester's rectangular ones and those at Caister-by-Norwich where semicircular forms appear beside rectangular ones. A tower at Caerwent has been dated not later than 350 but elsewhere they may not have been built until the fifth century, when the advice of Honorius would have been sufficient to hurry the laggardly into action. Strangely, no bastions are apparent at Wroxeter although aerial photographs show the late, wide town ditch diverging as though to accommodate them. Were bastions too costly for a small community lumbered with such a long perimeter? Were the fourth-century defences unfinished?

The investigation of bastions is hampered by the inadequacy of dating evidence. Once the variety of imported samian ware gave way to local fine wares the value of pottery for dating decreased sharply. With the breakdown of regular contact with the continent there would have been a loss of stimulus to innovation; and mid fourth-century forms could have continued for many decades. We have not so far recognized native products in the west that compare with the hand-made vessels found in late Roman or sub-Roman contexts in eastern Britain. There, Frere has estimated that the large potteries came to an end by about 420 through the loss of security for goods in transit and the escape of slaves once Imperial law collapsed. It is not known whether the Severn valley potteries continued through changes of government but they could not have survived for long. The shortage of coins became so acute that by 430 they were no longer in general use. Britain went back to bartering and there must have been a resultant reduction in the size of producer units.

Without coins or distinctive pottery we are left with only structural evidence. Only at Wroxeter, of the border towns, has there been extensive excavation aimed specifically at the recovery of post-Roman buildings. On the site of the demolished baths' basilica, in an area widely explored by Wright in the nineteenth century, Barker's interpretation of the post-basilican levels involves rectangular timber buildings, some on a massive scale and others like small cells against remnants of the basilica. These are held to represent the survival of the classical building tradition after the knowledge and skills of stone construction had been lost. They have been distinguished mainly by variations in wear and materials in the rubble surface on which they were identified. They lack any consistent foundation features so that the interpretation is inevitably extremely speculative. It involves too many unusual explanations to prove the occupation of Wroxeter in the Dark Ages.

This is not to say that the occupation of the city into the fifth century is unlikely. The six lead-weighted darts, plumbatae, found mostly around the baths' basilica are a type used by some legions in the fourth century and might be referred to Theodosius' campaign following the raids of 367. There are coins of the house of Valentinian, 364-83, from above the ruined market-hall colonnade but none later than 367 from the basilica site. In all the published finds from Wroxeter there are only three coins which must be later than 394, coins of Arcadius, emperor of the Eastern Empire, 395-408.

We are equally at a loss to document the last years of Kenchester and Caerwent. Excavations at Kenchester have produced no coins necessarily minted later than 383 but they include a coin of Theodosius I (379-95). From Caerwent there are coins of Arcadius and Honorius, minted between 393 and 423. Other evidence for the end of Roman life in these towns is rare and its significance disputed. The occasional skeletons found within the towns, for example beside the roads at Wroxeter and Caerwent, may have been victims of disease left unburied by a community that had lost its civic sense of responsibility; but are more likely late burials in graves rendered unrecognizable by root or plough action. Disease may have played a part in making the towns unattractive and ungovernable; but to stress this is to belittle the undoubted resistance of the Britons to the English advance which took some 200 years to reach the Severn.

The British opposition was probably directed from the west, from Wales and the Marches with which are associated the two best known Britons of the fifth century. The northern border and North Wales is thought to be the homeland of Vortigern, probably self-appointed as a leader around 425. He has been seen as the head of the groups accepting the Pelagian heresy, insisting on the right of individuals to decide their own fate, which in a political context meant without the aid of a Roman official. The other, Ambrosius Aurelianus, was a Roman noble linked by name to the family of the Catholic Bishop of Milan, and a supporter of the old regime and its system of patronage. He is thought to have had his special field of influence, if not kingdom, in the lands of the Severn estuary, in modern Gwent, Gloucestershire and Somerset.

Vortigern, himself the son-in-law of Magnus Maximus, must have had special reason to be grateful for the victory won by St Germanus over the Picts and Saxons in 429, probably in North Wales. Following this, and in order to remove the threat of Irish settlers in north-west Wales, Vortigern brought in frontier folk from south Scotland, the Votadini under the command of Cunedda. They may have used Chester as a base for their successful attack on the Irish. About the same time Vortigern invited the Saxon mercenaries under Hengist and Horsa to settle on Thanet as a shield against Pictish raids.

The Saxons advance to the Severn

More friendly relations had developed with the Irish who had settled in Wales in the late fourth and early fifth centuries; now, with Cunedda's help in the North, a *modus vivendi* had been established, permitting the Celtic west to maintain its traditional links with western Gaul and by that route with the church in Rome. The Irish connection is illustrated by a re-used tombstone from near Wroxeter that carries the crudely cut inscription CUNORIX MACUS MAQUI COLINE, translated as 'the Hound King (or Great King) Son of the Son of the Holly', an Irish name with a style that suggests a leader. Originally thought to be fifth century, it is now regarded as somewhat later.

Vortigern was probably succeeded as first war-lord of Britain some time after 443 by Ambrosius Aurelianus. The new leader was succeeded in his turn by a hero like the legendary King Arthur, whose medieval fictional exploits and chivalrous attributes appear to have been attached to a British war-leader rather than king of this time. He was probably the one who defeated the Saxons at Mount Badon about 500-516. By then organized town life at Verulamium, where new water pipes had been laid as late as 450, was at an end.

There is no comparable structural evidence for fifth-century survival at Kenchester or Caerwent. The basilica at Caerwent was destroyed by fire, though this would not preclude an urban existence. The town also lacks the late fifth-century Mediterranean pottery that is common in south-west England and appears in Wales on the fortified camps of Dinas Powys in Glamorgan, Coygan Camp in Dyfed and Dinas Emrys in Gwynedd.

The crude earthenware from the Breidden, Old Oswestry and Eddisbury Camps which was once thought to be Dark Age pottery is now seen to be Iron Age: either ordinary coarse ware as at Eddisbury or salt container fabric at Old Oswestry and the Breidden. This leaves a small sherd from Goodrich resembling imported Mediterranean Aii wares as the only pottery from the border to date from the fifth or sixth century.

Caerwent and Kenchester would have had little attraction or vitality once the Roman officials had been ousted but the regional units named after them and Wroxeter, survived the fifth century. Caerwent gave us the Kingdom of Gwent, and Magnis may possibly have perpetuated a district name, Mage, adopted by the Magonsaete who inhabited Herefordshire and south Shropshire. Viroconium, rather than the Wrekin, is the probable source for the Wroecensaete tribal name. The Kingdom of Erging derived its name from Ariconium. However the land was redistributed between Celt and Saxon, these names suggest some kind of accommodation between invader and resident.

The Celtic saints

Although Christianity was officially recognized in 313 the old gods remained popular, as the Romano-Celtic temple boom of the late fourth century proves. The conversion of the mass of the population came after the Roman withdrawal and was stimulated by a new generation of priests whose origins were partly Romano-British but who were also influenced by ideas reintroduced to Britain via the western sea routes from southern Gaul, or derived from the Celtic church in Ireland and west Wales. Many churches and chapels were founded by members of this church during the sixth and seventh centuries but north of the Wye the English rededicated most churches. Even in truly Welsh areas some churches would have been rededicated long after their foundation.

The archaeological evidence regarding the activities of these Celtic saints in the border is nil. It is not even clear whether we should anticipate any particular form of settlement accompanying or develop-

Plate 17 Early medieval memorial stones in Llanveynoe Church. The
inscriptions at the top of the right-hand stone read XPC, M (?Ω)
and IHC; and at the side HAEFDUR FECIT CRUCEM, IHC AΩ

ing upon the site of a Celtic church. Nor do we know from local
examples what these churches were like for they are probably buried
by their Norman successors.

One effect of this evangelical period was to emphasize the
separateness of certain parts of the border from the pagan English
lowland and from other Celtic Christian regions to the west. Considerable Romano-British survival, or later nostalgia, in Erging may be

indicated by the dedications to Saint Dubricius, or Dyfrig, who had the attributes of a Roman priest, embodying the respect for the Empire earlier shown by Ambrosius Aurelianus. The chapel of Dubricius, perhaps near Buckenhill Farm, Woolhope where a piscina was found, might indicate that Erging once extended east of the Wye. Other Celtic saints with dedications in Erging include Dewi, or David at Dewchurch and Kilpeck, and Beuno at Llanveynoe, in which church is a Christian memorial stone of the eleventh or twelfth century, similar to several found around St David's, Dyfed. Beside it is a crucifixion stone of the same period (pl 17). Cadog, the most popular early saint in Gwent, was similarly steeped in Roman tradition.

It is in such areas, if anywhere, that we might expect continuity from the Romano-British scene and some attempt to maintain a supply of pottery. If the factories had closed we might expect domestic manufacture based on fourth-century models and the looting of military cemeteries for vessels of any period. Either way, the pots in use round early churches or settlements will be difficult to distinguish in form from those deposited in late Roman times. Where grave vessels were employed they could be centuries older than the Dark Age deposits yielding them. Despite the uncertainties of the alleged Celtic saint foundations, there must be a case for investigating the vicinity of such churches. Just south of St Dubricius' church, Hentland, timber structures, ditches and Romano-British sherds, were found beneath the level of medieval buildings.

Even north of the Wye the rivers retain their British names like Frome, Lugg, Severn and Teme, and Welsh elements are sometimes found in place-names, but there are few dedications to Celtic saints. Nevertheless the church at Leominster, Welsh Llanllieni, was founded by Dewi and Kenchester was once dedicated to the Celtic saint Keyna.

There is a notable cluster of dedications to St Tysilio in northern Powys against the national boundary and a similar juxtaposition of boundary and dedications to Beuno and other Celtic saints occurs in the upper Severn between Berriew and Guilsfield. Further north the descendants of Coel Godebog and Cunedda appear in half a dozen dedications between Llangollen and Bangor-on-Dee; and St Beuno, along with his associated saints, is well represented around Whitford.

The struggle for the border; to AD 800

While the pressure on the southern border was from the West Saxons, the threat in the north was from Northumbria. In the late sixth century the northern border enjoyed the protection of Urien of Rheged who was fighting against the Northumbrians in the 570s. With the English victory at Chester in 614 and the subsequent march of Edwin into North Wales the security of the Severn valley and the farmlands around Wroxeter was placed in jeopardy. This may have been the occasion for the abandonment of Wroxeter in favour of a smaller, more easily defended site, perhaps the Berth hillfort near Baschurch, or the nucleus of Shrewsbury, where the Severn offers defence on three sides. The only dating evidence to support either of these is a bronze cauldron pierced for use as a waterclock and dug up in the marsh that formerly surrounded the Berth. Such cauldrons are thought to be Dark Age but the device is widespread and the dates of particular examples uncertain. There is ceramic evidence that the Berth was occupied in the Iron Age and Roman periods. The issue of a successor to Wroxeter dogs the discussion of ensuing events in the Severn valley. The response to the Northumbrian invasion was the alliance of Penda of Mercia and Cadwallon of Gwynedd which resulted in the defeat of Edwin in 632. But ten years later the northerners under Oswald were again campaigning in the Marches. Again they were beaten, and Oswald killed, at Maserfelth, uncertainly located in Shropshire and argued to be an earlier name for Oswestry which itself means 'Oswald's tree (or cross)'. Penda's death in 654 disrupted Mercia. The Magonsaete settled the border from the Wrekin to the Wye and there was a resurgence of British resistance in the northern Marches.

Among the sources for this period are the poems of Llywarch Hen, a late sixth-century king of Lancashire who fled to Powys when the English conquered his land. He tells of the exploits of a seventh-century hero Cynddylan, son of Cyndrwyn, who raided the English and lived in a great hall at Pengwern in the white town by the woods. Morris suggested that Cynddylan's abode was Viroconium, the plastered buildings of which would have befitted the 'white town' of the poem. Richards has argued for the Wrekin, mentioned as 'Dinlleu Vreconn' but the windswept hill is hardly appropriate for the 'head of the alder grove' which is what Pengwern means. In the thirteenth century Giraldus Cambrensis equated Pengwern with Shrewsbury but the British name for that town was Amwythig. The edge of the marsh at the Berth would have been a suitable habitat for alder, and only a mile from Baschurch where Cynddylan was buried. Lastly, the poet's location of Cynddylan's home being between 'Tren and Trodwydd', thought to be Tern and Roden, raises the possibility of the large hillfort of Bury Walls. The poet himself may have been confused.

Archaeology had been silent on the matter of the early English settlement but at Bromfield in 1978 an Anglo-Saxon Christian cemetery

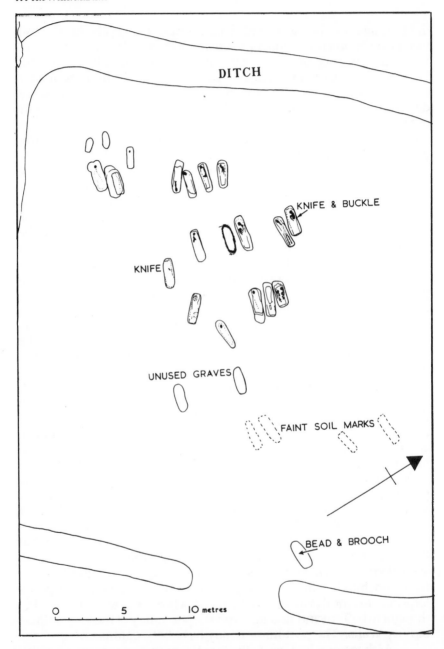

Fig 43 The Saxon cemetery within the abandoned Iron Age farm at Bromfield

was excavated within the Iron Age farmstead enclosure (p 55). Traces of up to thirty-one graves were found, orientated roughly east-west and all but three devoid of grave goods (fig 43). Two burials with small Anglo-Saxon knives, and one with a bronze brooch and amber bead just inside the entrance, identify the occupants and point to a continuance of pagan English customs. There could be an earlier pagan cemetery nearby but the barrow I formerly thought might belong to it is now seen to be pre-Roman. The cemetery should date to the period 650-750 when similar sites were in use over much of Saxon England and be contemporary with the cemetery of seven inhumation graves within a barrow excavation area on the Long Mountain at Trelystan. Both sites show the recently converted Saxons, or perhaps Britons at the Welsh site, burying their dead in the vicinity of earlier burial mounds: at Bromfield even within an ancient earthwork. The growing power of the Church was soon able to draw them away from such pagan reminders and require burial in its own ground. At Bromfield that would have been the Priory Church, just across the river.

The period between the arrival of the Saxons in the Marches and their conversion to Christianity around 650 would have been less than fifty years but a few place-names hint at pagan burial mounds. Wolferlow in north-east Herefordshire means 'Wulfhere's tumulus'; and Gelling lists seven widely spread in Shropshire: Beslow, Longslow, Munslow, Onslow, Peplow, Purslow and Whittingslow. Other English place-names dominate the map, eloquent of the way in which Anglo-Saxon culture replaced the British from the Mersey to the Wye and overspilled into Erging or Archenfield. It even penetrated the central hills and reached into the Vale of Radnor.

By the time the English entered the Marches they already had a wide repertoire of place-name forms to draw upon and their quick over-running of the area means that almost any place-name type may be widespread within something like a county area but be rare in a neighbouring county. There may a hint of such a contrast between Shropshire and Herefordshire in the pagan 'low' names just discussed. Again, names ending originally in '-ham' (village) as distinct from 'hamm' (river-meadow), seem to be rare south of Cheshire where Dodgson regards them as indicative of the earliest stage of English settlement in the seventh century. Aside from possibly documenting the English settlement they portray the contemporary landscape.

In particular they reflect the continuing importance of the Roman roads and the survival of forested areas from the Iron Age. Thus there is a concentration of names in '-ley' and '-field' in the west Herefordshire plain: Almeley, Eardisley and Sarnesfield among them. Across it, following the gravel terrace of the Wye, went the road to

Clyro, and along the road are places with names in '-ton' like Winforton, Staunton, Letton and Monnington. Similarly taking over existing clearings, the English planted their 'tons' along the road to Gloucester at Preston, Aylton, Ashperton and Stretton Grandison. Away from the road, names like Putley, Pixley, Munsley and the Marcles mark settlements in partly forested areas. More such names predominate around Leintwardine, where too there had been much Roman activity. Letton, Burrington, Adforton and Buckton are among them.

Over most of Herefordshire, however, there is a mixture of name types including many topographical names in '-hope', meaning valley, and '-ford'. Others, like the several Fromes, used British river names. Marden and Maund in the Lugg valley may, like Roman Magnis, derive from a possible district name, Mage, perhaps meaning rocks or stone, though there are difficulties with these names as Gelling has detailed. Around Leominster, the element 'land', in Eardisland, Kingsland and others, recalls the pre-Domesday hundred of Lene which may have originated in a British district.

Such survivals may imply that the eventual political map was not the result of conflict between Welsh and English neighbours but rather a common acquiescence to the military power of Mercia. The original groups of English adventurers like the Magonsaete and Hwicce, who moved into Herefordshire across the Malverns, established their own enclaves in the late sixth and early seventh centuries; but by 693 the Diocese of Hereford had been founded and the region brought under Mercian control. What was left of an independent British culture was mostly blanketed by the uniformity of an alien language and separate religious organization. Nevertheless, the Domesday recognition of Welsh custom in parts of Herefordshire and the record of Welshmen even north of the Wye, hints that below this foreign veneer some British communities survived to integrate slowly and help form the border's own culture, neither lowland English nor upland Welsh.

The broken terrain of south Shropshire, where the colonists had to feel their way between the hills, was not amenable to settlement in broad successive zones; but there are glimpses of nuclear areas with names in '-ton'. On the watershed south of Much Wenlock are found Bourton, Acton Round and Monkhopton; similar names spill southwest into Corve Dale focusing attention on the probable Roman origin of the road, close to which stand Shipton and Stanton Long, and the possible pagan-phase settlement of Munslow (p 115).

Northwards, beyond the river gravels of the Severn, '-ton' names are much less common, with names in '-ley' and '-field' showing that much of the Ellesmere moraine and its margins was still wooded. Beyond the moraine the names of Cheshire villages are strikingly different, marking a different source of colonists. West of the Weaver there are no fewer than eleven names in '-ington', and one in '-ingham', which contain personal names, notably rare to the south in Shropshire. Together with names in '-ton' they far outnumber the topographical names in '-ley' etc.

The impression of early and intensive English settlement of this area, which extends for a few miles west of the Dee between Wrexham and Hawarden, is in accord with the historical record of the Northumbrian capture of Chester, opening the area to English settlers during the first decades of the seventh century. For a while the infertile lands of the Ellesmere moraine saved the British communities in the Severn valley from coming under pressure from the north but by then the English were probably already in Herefordshire. So for a generation or two the Celtic and English provinces alternated through the Marches. Gwent and Erging remained Welsh, though English conquests across the Wye reduced the size and viability of the latter kingdom. The English held Herefordshire and the vanguard was ready to push into the Vale of Radnor. With the northern plains also under English control, Shropshire may have been the scene of a rearguard action for British survival involving places like Oswestry, the Berth, Shrewsbury and Wroxeter. One of the probable results of this laggardly submission was that Shrewsbury acquired no cathedral and the dioceses of Hereford and Lichfield shared Shropshire between them.

Archaeological evidence is lacking for the conflict of these years, whether military or cultural. Nor is it likely to be found close to present-day settlements, even though they may bear pre-Domesday names. The Bromfield cemetery prepares us for the probable movement of even the Saxon villages, along with their cemeteries. About 800, reorganization brought the population of much of England to lower, fertile ground from the often marginal heaths they had previously occupied. Later, there might still be an ongoing shift of farms and cottages such as Wade-Martins has demonstrated in East Anglia. The older, if not the oldest, site may be expected close to the parish church, the most stable element. Unfortunately, the large farms and houses of the modern village are also often close to the church and the surface deeply eroded by hollow ways and stockyards. In such circumstances the chances of discovering Dark Age traces are remote. We need sites which disappeared before or very soon after the Norman conquest which may mean dispensing with churches as guide-posts and searching on the basis of earthwork alone. The normal shortage of pottery in the Marches will render the task all the more difficult. Furthermore the reason for the desertion of many medieval villages was that they lay on marginal land, difficult to cultivate and most sensitive to adverse fluctuations of climate because of their altitude or poor drainage. They were themselves secondary settlements from the fat lands that were the subject of the swarming of AD 800. Their excavation would not unveil the seventh-century pioneers.

If we can locate these early settlements and their valleyward successors intact we might learn the origins of the medieval timber-framed houses that decorate the Marches; and perhaps see whether, somewhat unlikely, they stemmed from the rectangular timber huts of the hillforts, for single-cell structures no larger than the hillfort dwellings are still to be found in the border. Two obvious differences are that the surviving post-medieval buildings have stone chimneys and are based on sleeper beams instead of ground-fast posts.

The question of population replacement might just possibly be settled by an abandoned cemetery with bones still preserved, requiring a site with alkaline soil, perhaps near the limestone of Wenlock Edge, or the hills around Wigmore.

The Mercian boundary dykes

The expansion of English power during the seventh and eighth centuries brought the new settlers to the banks of the Wye in the south and the front of the Cambrian Massif elsewhere. By the end of that period local frontier works had been built to defend the enlarged English kingdom against Welsh resurgence.

The most extensive system of linear earthworks in Britain is named after Offa, King of Mercia 757-96, whose frontier, using a combination of rivers and artificial dykes, ran from the mouth of the Wye to the estuary of the Dee. This marked the culmination of frontier defences in the west and is thought to have followed the use of other, more easterly, dykes like Wat's Dyke, attributed to Aethelbald 716-57, and the Rowe Ditch. It is difficult to guess the date of a number of other shorter, cross-ridge and cross-valley dykes west of Offa's line. They are generally thought to belong to the early years of Mercian expansion, perhaps to the reigns of Penda, 626-55, or Wulfhere, 656-75, though some might be outworks of Offa's system; and even prehistoric or later medieval dates cannot be ruled out.

Wat's Dyke (fig 44)

This earthwork forms, with a number of streams, a line between the Afon Vyrnwy and the Dee estuary. Like the other dykes it consists of a single bank thrown up from a western ditch, set where possible on a west-facing slope, and clearly an English construction against the Welsh. It incorporates as many kilometres as possible of the deep ravines that trench the northern plains, thereby acquiring the strong positions appropriate to a defensive line along a frontier, between one and six kilometres east of Offa's Dyke.

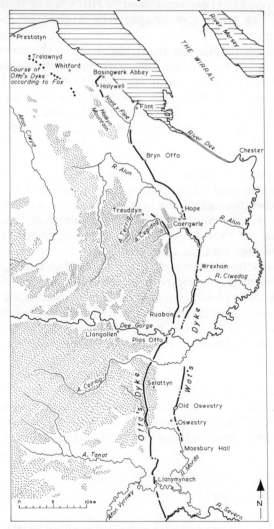

Fig 44 Offa's Dyke and Wat's Dyke in the
northern Marches (sources Fox 1955
and Hill 1974) Land over 250m stippled

It lies regularly along the divide between English and Welsh names but the apparently Welsh names between the two dykes include many, like Selattyn and Brogyntyn, that are English names modified by Welsh re-occupation. Wat's Dyke must have still been in fair condition for the Welsh advance to have halted along it - an argument for its being behind the settlement frontier, just as Offa's Dyke was shown to be by Noble. This point has been reinforced by Hill's demonstration that the gaps in the dyke, which Fox thought to be original, are the result of later levelling.

The eastern dyke ran from Holywell to the river Morda, a tributary of the Vyrnwy, which joins the Severn near the Breidden. As dyke or ravine it is continuous northwards to the Nant y Flint, which flows into the Dee at Flint. Fox regarded this town as the natural terminus for this frontier but proposed that the dyke continued, albeit intermittently, another six kilometres to Holywell and Basingwerk Abbey, beyond the area of predominantly English place-names. He thus rejected the local naming of the dyke here as Clawdd Offa and a fourteenth-century reference to Basingwerk as the end of Offa's Dyke.

Fox was clearly influenced by his conviction that Offa's Dyke itself was to be traced along the hills to terminate near Prestatyn. His evidence for this was slight and Hill's excavations at Trelawnyd and west of Whitford found no dyke along its suggested course. The historical evidence for Offa's Dyke ending at Basingwerk must therefore stand, with the dyke brought down to the plain to adopt the earlier frontier between the Terrig-Alun confluence and the Nant y Flint where Wat's Dyke closed to the sea. The extension north-west from here to Holywell gave closer protection to more English land, as was the case wherever Offa's line diverged from the earlier one.

The frontier defined by Wat's Dyke bounds the territory of the northern plains and by way of Old Oswestry closes with the left bank tributaries of the Severn, the Morda and Vyrnwy. Parish boundaries coincide with only about 13% of the known course. Allowing for some later reorganization, it looks as though the dyke was, in this respect too, similar to Offa's Dyke as re-interpreted by Noble: a military conception securing the best line of defence behind the ragged edge of pioneering acquisitions.

The Rowe Ditch (fig 45)

This earthwork is in the same longitudinal position as Wat's Dyke but its shortness and topographical siting is reminiscent of the western cross-dykes. It crosses the flood plain of the Arrow near Pembridge,

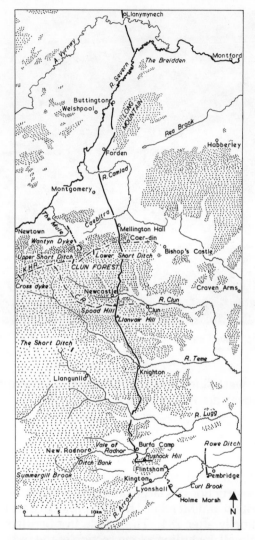

Fig 45 Offa's Dyke and the short dykes
in the central Marches (Fox 1955)
CR Clun Ridgeway KHR Kerry Hill
Ridgeway. Stippling: over 250m

five kilometres east of Offa's Dyke and four kilometres long (pl 19).
Fox saw it as a barrier across the cleared valley land, closing the gap
between a forest to the south and hills to the north. Where preserved,
it consists of a single bank up to fifteen metres wide, thrown up from

Plate 19   The Rowe Ditch, much reduced, at the Leen, Pembridge

a ditch on the west side. With an obvious defensive capability, it offered a causeway across the often flooded valley.

Offa's Dyke

In the ninth century Bishop Asser described Offa as the king who 'ordered the construction of a large rampart the whole way from sea to sea between Britain and Mercia'. The conventional date for the start of this work is shortly after 784. The whole frontier, from the Severn estuary to Holywell, including a long section of the river Wye and the gaps in west Herefordshire, was about 226 kilometres. On this line south of Treuddyn there still stands 120 kilometres of earthwork, equivalent to the ramparts of seventy-five Midsummer Hill camps. Although it was a unitary scheme of defence between English and Welsh, it took in several very different sectors each with its own topographical, economic and political problems. Some of these differences had their origins earlier in the post-Roman period when the Romanized south had special links with the Irish church, whereas northerners had been brought into the Dee basin to check Irish incursions. The mixture of cultures along the Wye contrasted with the imposition of a powerful Anglian supremacy in Cheshire. The situations confronting politicians and frontier engineers varied, and so consequently did their solutions.

Fox interpreted the line of Offa's Dyke as a compromise boundary, favouring Mercian interests since Offa would have been the more powerful party in the negotiations. So, although the dyke generally achieved a course looking down on Wales, Offa was thought to have compromised by leaving the Welsh in occupation of some lands already secured by English settlers. Noble's study of the problem, edited by Gelling, convincingly re-interpreted the frontier. Discovering that the dyke crosses most townships indifferently, Noble realized that the dyke must be later than the townships, so had not normally been set at the western limit of colonization. The main cases of boundary and dyke coincidence are in old Montgomeryshire where the English had regained lost land after Offa's time. Virtually the only circumstance in which one can imagine an apparent frontier work lying behind the national frontier would be if the military were given full rein to put their defence work in the most defensive position compatible with national territory and financial restrictions. In this way was Offa's Maginot Line built. It did not represent the limit of English colonization in 784; it left some settlements to the west unprotected but did not thereby forfeit them to the Welsh. The diocese of Hereford, which must have been established well before Offa's time, never lost jurisdiction over townships west of the dyke.

North of Herefordshire, Offa's Dyke lies on the edge of the highlands (fig 44) claiming the whole of the lowlands for Mercia. Fox thought that the many gaps north of Treuddyn reflected a lack of labour in a thinly populated area but it is clear that more earthwork has been ploughed down than he appreciated. South of Treuddyn the work becomes the massive bank with western ditch that it exhibits for most of its course. Constructed across broken ground west of Wrexham it runs via Ruabon to the lower end of the Dee gorge. Striking across hill and valley to the high ground north-west of Selattyn, it is brought downhill west of Oswestry and then follows the sides of Llanymynech Hill to the plain of the Vyrnwy, and so to the Severn.

Along the whole sector from Treuddyn to Llanymynech the dyke is roughly parallel to Wat's Dyke and has a similarly forthright course with few alignments. It leaves little ground below 250 metres to the west and roughly marks the western limit of intensive arable farming. The economic and military potential of the Welsh was further reduced. At the end of this stretch, in Powys, the whole situation is different, for the Cambrian front is neither so abrupt nor high and an extensive area of cultivable land remained Welsh. Just here in fact, where one might expect the population to have been considerable on both sides, the Offan frontier makes little military sense (fig 45). The Severn itself, a meandering and fluctuating stream in these reaches, served as the line for eight kilometres from near the Breidden to the vicinity of Buttington near Welshpool. Thence a bank climbs obliquely to the top south-west corner of the Long Mountain, only to descend again to the plain near Forden and curve south across the Camlad to reach the foot of the hills at Mellington Hall. By maintaining its direct, shorter course it left unprotected to the west English settlements like Hopton which were only shielded by the Wantyn cross-valley dyke.

Offa's Dyke now enters its mountain zone, between 360 and 426 metres, on the uplands of Clun Forest. It uses westward facing slopes as much as possible and diverges when necessary to gain suitable hills from which new alignments may be sighted. Nowhere is it more splendidly constructed or more brilliantly conceived than in this long stretch from the Powys border to Herefordshire. Crossing the Kerry Hill ridgeway route, it demonstrates that one of its functions was to prevent ridge-top movement, whether of soldiers or cattle rustlers. No sector is neglected. Though locally based enemies may have been few, the danger lay further afield in the heart of Wales; and that way, south-west along the ridge, lie short cross-dykes at points where the approach of steep tributary dingles creates easily defended waists along the route. The first, the Lower Short Ditch, lies some four kilometres west of Offa's Dyke at about 457 metres; it is 730 metres long with a western ditch. Three kilometres further west, at the next waist, is the Upper Short Ditch, at the same altitude and about as long, commanding the junction of the Clun and Kerry Hill ridgeways. Just west of this the present Shropshire boundary marks the limit of English interest in the mountain zone.

Eight kilometres west again, and now fifteen kilometres west of Offa's Dyke, lies a third cross-ridge dyke at the western end of Kerry Hill. It is difficult to regard a work as far west as this as constructed by early English settlers; but equally it is difficult to divorce it in function from the other two cross-ridge dykes. All three may have served as customs barriers but could belong to brief episodes of conflict, thrown up by an English army against the threat of pursuit from Wales. In connection with them Fox drew attention to Caer-din, a univallate rectilinear earthwork of 0.8 hectare, on the Kerry Hill ridge a kilometre east of Offa's Dyke; Musson and Spurgeon have mooted the possibility of a line of forts along the frontier.

Leading south over this dissected plateau, the dyke crosses the

Clun valley below Newcastle, climbs over Spoad Hill and Llanvair Hill and reaches the Teme gorge at Knighton. Taking an awkward course across lowland and hill it enters an English salient in the Vale of Radnor. There it zigzags around the eastern rim of the vale to leave a large area of English place-names to the west. Soon, on Rushock Hill, it turns its back on upland Wales and looks upon Herefordshire.

In the Vale of Radnor another area of English settlement was left to the west. As in the Wantyn Brook area, the excluded territory was protected by a short dyke further into Wales. Ten kilometres west of Offa's Dyke and only two south-west of New Radnor, Ditch Bank crosses the valley of the Summergill Brook. It looks as though these settlers were provided with local defence although they were excluded by the national dyke, support again for Noble's thesis. A last ridge-dyke, the Short Ditch, crosses an important route north-west of Llangunllo, spanning the ridge between the heads of deeply incised dingles.

Between Rushock Hill and the Wye at Bridge Sollers there are only short sectors preserved across the main valleys. That of the Arrow is crossed between Flintsham Farm and the opposing river cliffs which offer a stretch of natural defence. Then, starting near Lyonshall, a large bank crosses the valley of the Curl Brook (pl 20).

There is then a considerable gap along the watershed of the Lugg and Wye drainage before the Yazor Brook section is reached. Fox thought a dyke unnecessary here on account of dense oakwoods. These poorly drained plains had probably never been extensively cultivated; no Iron Age or Roman settlements occur there. This was therefore a desert where lack of Welsh pressure made the dyke unnecessary. The English settlement of Herefordshire had pressed along the valleys, where extensive spreads of sand and gravel offered better drained soils and the dyke had only to cover these intakes as far as intensive settlement had gone. Beyond the valley dykes place-names in '-ley' and '-wood' confirm the forested nature of the area, claimed by the English but only sparsely settled. Short stretches of dyke occur on either side of the Yazor Brook. Then the last stretch before the Wye crosses the plain at its narrowest, south of Garnons Hill, a choice that emphasizes its military purpose.

For ninety-six kilometres, from Bridge Sollers to the highest limit of tide near Redbrook, the Wye was probably both defence and frontier. Fox thought that half a kilometre of broken work south of the river at English Bicknor might be Offan. Sometimes invoked are the Row Ditches at Hereford and a bank and ditches at Perrystone Court, Foy. The latter is an uncertain earthwork which Fox thought might be a pre-Offan boundary. The Hereford Row Ditches are medieval, not the

Plate 20   Offa's Dyke, crowned by oaks, on the east side of the Curl Brook

work of Offa, nor the Scots' army as shown on old Ordnance Survey maps.

On the south-west side of this alleged frontier, marked by a river that is fordable in several places, English place-names are mixed with Welsh ones. Their settlements will not be post-Offan and we must conclude that the river was regarded as a cheap and reasonable line of defence, at least for the time being.

South of Redbrook the dyke reappears, high on the eastern cliffs of the Wye, only occasionally descending to cross re-entrant valleys, and occasionally being omitted where the cliffs were particularly steep. From Dennel Hill, Tidenham, the river cliffs were followed for three kilometres before a short stretch of dyke brought the frontier down with the cliff to the river bank just north of Chepstow. In this sector the defences of Spital Meend Camp were used, just as Wat's Dyke used those of Old Oswestry. From the vicinity of Chepstow the cliffs must have served as the defence until their end half a kilometre below the railway bridge. Here a cliff-top earthwork holding about 0.2 hectare was thought by Fox to be possibly related to the dyke but it could equally be Iron Age. The silted creek on its south side presumably served as the line for the first 250 metres across the Beachley peninsula

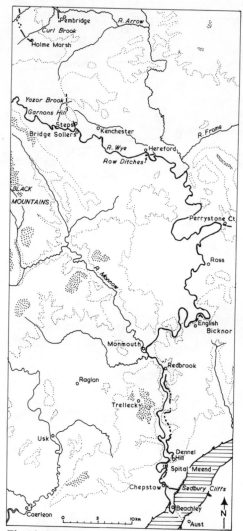

Fig 46 Offa's Dyke in the south (Fox 1955)
120m contour dotted. Land over 250m
stippled

but a dyke defines the last kilometre to Sedbury Cliffs where the great
Mercian defence line terminated.

The construction of dykes to connect lengths of river cliff downstream from Redbrook instead of using the river as a frontier was
explained by Fox in terms of land concessions to the Welsh, acknowl-
edging their presumed ancient interests in Beachley port, northern

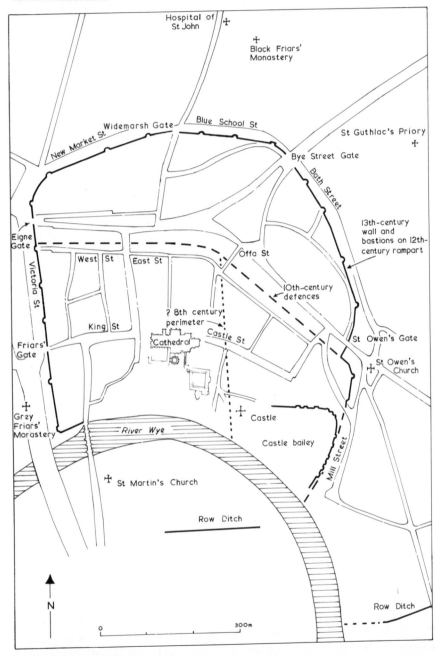

Fig 47 The defences of Hereford (Sources Taylor 1786 and Shoesmith 1975)

terminus of the Aust ferry, and navigation to the limit of spring tides on the Wye, requiring control of both banks of the river. The reinterpretation of Offa's line purely as a military concept was backed by Noble's re-assessment of the early history of Tidenham manor which extended, like most others, both sides of the dyke. It is easy so see why the Mercian army preferred the top of the river cliffs to the banks of the meandering Wye or the shore of the Severn. In front of their line, continued English occupation ensured the English character of the east bank of the Wye and of the Beachley peninsula.

East and north of the Wye the border was thus formally declared to be under Mercian control. Most of the land south of that river remained in the Welsh kingdoms of Gwent and Erging, probably with some special relationship between English and Welsh in the latter. The Marches in general were to provide a battleground where the rivalries of English and Welsh princes could be settled, a buffer against Welsh attack, a springboard for English assault.

It is appropriate that such an important political and cultural watershed should now be used as the major part of a national footpath, the Offa's Dyke path, originally designated in 1955 but only coming into use as a result of the energetic advocacy of Noble and others in the 1960s. From Sedbury Cliffs to Fox's conjectural terminal at Prestatyn it offers a fine introduction to the border.

After Offa

While English and Welsh struggled to extend their power at each other's expense, the Vikings threw in their contribution to the chaos of the late ninth and tenth centuries. Their raids in the Severn estuary have left no recognizable monuments, nor is much known about the fortified settlements, known as burhs, established against them. Along the Severn the main bridgepoints at Gloucester, Worcester, Bridgnorth and Shrewsbury were guarded by burhs. The one at Shrewsbury was in existence as early as 901 when it was recorded in the Charter of Ethelred and Ethelfleda; its mint is marked on issues of Athelstan, 925-939, and his successors until the Norman Conquest. Since mints could only operate in defended places, ports or burhs, from the tenth century onwards, the town must have remained fortified. The Shrewsbury burh probably occupied the highest part of town, as shown by the late Saxon Chester ware found at 2A St Alkmund's Place. The castle area must have been developed; there is mention of fifty-one houses being destroyed there when the outer bailey was added by Earl Roger of Montgomery between 1074 and 1086.

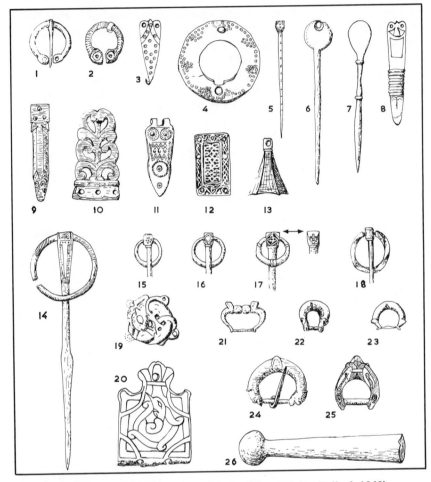

Fig 48 Dark Age bronze objects from Meols, Wirral (After Bu'lock 1960)
All x1/2

1 & 2 Sub-Roman pennanular brooches
3 Belt hook, probably eighth century
4 Anglo-Saxon annular brooch
5 Faceted pin, seventh-ninth century
6 & 7 Disc-headed pins, eighth-tenth century
8-10 Strap ends, ninth-eleventh century
11 Buckle plate
12 Mount, eighth-ninth century
13 Six-sided bell
14-18 Ring-headed pins, seventh-eleventh century
19 Mount with intertwining animals, eighth-ninth century
20 Mount, tenth-eleventh century
21-25 Zoomorphic buckles, ninth-twelfth century
26 Viking drinking-horn mount terminal

In 914 Ethelfleda built a burh at Eddisbury, presumably re-occupying the hillfort, and in 915 another at 'Cyricbyrig', thought to be Chirbury. A rectangular enclosure, Chirbury Castle, in the north-west corner of the village may have been the site of this burh but excavations found no palisade, defensive ditch or internal occupation.

At Hereford, centre of the bishopric since the late seventh century, Mercia faced the Welsh in Erging, or Archenfield, and the two powers were locked in battle there in 760. The city's earliest rampart, built in the middle of the ninth century, has only been observed on the west side of the town beneath later ramparts beside Victoria Street and Berrington Street (fig 47). It may have followed West and East Streets before turning south, as Offa Street, towards the river. The earliest fortified town would then have been almost square, bisected by an east-west High Street along the line perpetuated by King Street and Castle Street. This rampart was enlarged and given a timber front revetment possibly in the early tenth century, the equivalent of the burh defences elsewhere. Certainly Hereford had burh status in 914 when the Danes were raiding Archenfield. By then the town extended east of Castle Green to the line of the later city wall beside Mill Street and enclosed about twenty-one hectares. Later in the tenth century the rampart was given a stone face. Earl Harold restored them again after the sack of the city in 1055 by Gruffydd ap Llywelyn aided by the Mercian Aelfgar.

Suburbs were probably already developing north of the town wall in the eleventh century. When the defences were next recon-structed, a gravel rampart enclosed them, establishing the line along New Market Street, Blue School Street and Bath Street. This probably followed the 1189 Charter for the fortification of the city which then extended to thirty-seven hectares. South of the Wye the Row Ditch protected the suburb of St Martin's and the bridgehead. The other Row Ditch north of the river shielded the arable land in Portfield. In the thirteenth century a stone wall was inserted in the front of the rampart but where it curved the masons preferred to work in straight sectors. Since the curve was not regular their changes of alignment were not equally spaced; so neither were the semicircular bastions which were built at these angles. Hereford's defences, with no fewer than six phases of fortification postulated between the ninth and thirteenth centuries, reflect the recurrence of Viking raids and Welsh pressure that forced the development of town fortifications.

Through most of the border there was no permanent legacy of the Danish raids. In the north, however, raids from bases in Ireland and the Isle of Man were accompanied by the settlement of the Wirral and Merseyside, distinguished by Norse place-names like West Kirby,

Whitby and Helsby. They were accompanied by missionary activity commemorated by Anglo-Norse wheel-shaped crosses evolved from Norse forms across the Irish Sea. They are found as far south as Chester but over the rest of Cheshire Mercian round-shaft crosses predominate.

The northern tip of the Wirral attracted seafarers and traders throughout the Dark Ages as it had done in prehistory. The numerous finds include belt fittings, annular brooches, a pottery flask of Mediterranean origin from the immediate post-Roman centuries and two Mercian coins of the late seventh or early eighth century. These and other finds (fig 48) attest the importance of the peninsula, particularly Whitby monastery and the port area of Meols, Hoylake and West Kirby. There was a gradual increase of Irish, and then Norse, trading and missionary activity over a long period, with most finds coming from the coast. The sea has bitten into old settlements and redistributed the land-spits which, until the nineteenth century, defined the Hoyle Lake lagoon and harbour.

Viking pressure on North Wales had restrained the ambition of Rodri Mawr, 844-78, King of Gwynedd, Powys and Seisyllwg against the kings of South Wales. When he died, his sons Anarawd and Cadell posed a threat to Gwent, Brycheiniog, Morgannwg, Rhwng Gwy a Hafren and Dyfed, causing their rulers to seek the help of Alfred, King of Wessex. In so doing they gave later English kings a precedent for their claims to be overlords in Wales. Though the country was briefly unified under Gruffydd ap Llywelyn, 1039-63, it fell into separate kingdoms again following his defeat and death when Earl Harold invaded North Wales in 1062-3. Gruffydd had raided as far as Chester, Leominster and Hereford but at his death the frontier was again close to that of Offa's day. The scene was set for the Norman invasion that was to alter the course of English social and political history.

CHAPTER NINE

Castles in the Marches

The Norman feudal system was based on military service; and the Welsh border country came under the heavy imprint of the professional soldier. Castles sprang up on every hand, from the major strategic centres of the king to the mottes that mushroomed in almost every western parish. The region had known before the defence-works of its hillfort farmers and the forts built to hold Roman imperial garrisons. It had known something too of the burhs, constructed by Anglo-Saxon princes for the benefit of the whole community. It was now to see the proliferation of strongholds designed as part of a professional war game to be waged against any rebellious English or against the Welsh, for the prime object of increasing personal wealth and prestige. Just as the social developments prompted or accelerated by the Conqueror's accession were to result in an increasing gulf between the governors and the governed, so too were the defence works of the military to impress a character of conflict and memory of bitterness upon the lands of the border and the valleys of Wales. The Marches' castles survive as frequent and cruel monuments to that phase in our history when the Anglo-Norman east became indelibly distinct from the Celtic west.

The stage for later conflict was already being prepared about 1050 with Edward the Confessor's infusion of Normans into the border. His nephew Ralph built the first castle at Hereford, while the Norman Osbern established the Lordship of Ewyas Harold in the Black Mountains and another Norman built a castle at 'Auretone' - Richard's Castle. Despite these preparations, Hereford was destroyed in 1055 and its defences had to be rebuilt by Harold Godwinson, Earl of Wessex, when he became Earl of Hereford. In view of Harold's great influence in the Marches it is not surprising that a Herefordshire thegn, Eadric the Wild, with Welsh princes as his allies, was one who rebelled against King William in 1069.

In 1071 the lowlands of the Dee, Severn and Wye were divided into the three earldoms of Chester, Shrewsbury and Hereford, to be defended by castles both in their own territory and forward in Wales (fig 49). Hugh d'Avranches was given Chester, with a forward castle at Rhuddlan under his cousin Robert. Robert of Montgomery became Earl of Shrewsbury with an outpost west of the dyke at Montgomery or, as Barker has argued, at Hen Domen, a small motte and bailey two kilometres to the north-west. William FitzOsbern, Earl of Hereford,

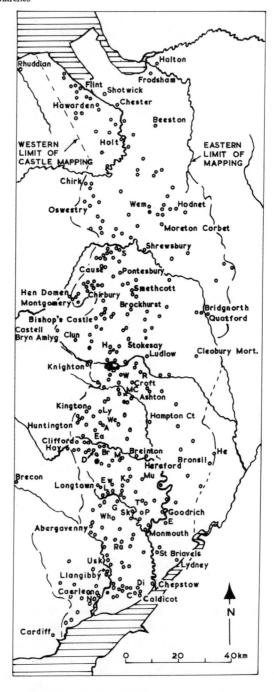

WESTERN
LIMIT OF
CASTLE MAPPING

EASTERN
LIMIT OF
MAPPING

Rhuddlan

Halton

Frodsham

Flint

Shotwick

Hawarden

Chester

Beeston

Holt

Chirk

Wem

Hodnet

Oswestry

Moreton Corbet

Shrewsbury

S

Cause

Pontesbury

Hen Domen

Chirbury

Smethcott

Montgomery

Brockhurst

Bridgnorth
Quatford

Bishop's Castle

Castell
Bryn Amlyg

Clun

Ho

Stokesay

Ludlow

Cleobury Mort.

Knighton

W

R

Croft

MC

Ashton

Kington

Ly

We

A

Hampton Ct

Huntington

Clifford

Ea

Hay

Br

M

Breinton

He

D

Bronsil

Hereford

Brecon

Longtown

E

W

K

Mu

L

T

G

Sk

P

Goodrich

Who

E

Abergavenny

Monmouth

Ra

St Briavels

Usk

Lydney

Llangibby

Di

Chepstow

Caerleon

No

C

Caldicot

Cardiff

N

0   20   40 km

defended the Wye basin with castles at Wigmore, Clifford and Ewyas Harold, and invaded Gwent to establish the Lordship of Striguil around Chepstow. By 1086 the Normans held Caerleon and the line of the Usk. In 1093, following the defeat of Rhys ap Tewdwr, they set up the Lordships of Glamorgan and Brecon. The sequence was that of the Roman conquest all over again.

From Montgomery, or Hen Domen, the Earl of Shrewsbury attacked Wales along the Severn valley to gain control of the Cantrefs of Cydewain and Arwystli, and the waist of Wales. From Oswestry the Normans pressed north-westwards; and from Chester, moved quickly along the coast, establishing castles at Deganwy, Conway and Caernarvon.

The ensuing Norman campaigns, Welsh resistance and rebellion, led to a long sequence of castle building at the cost of much energy and wealth to render them secure against improving methods of attack. Quite elaborate works were still being undertaken four centuries after the first Norman infiltration of the border.

The most important sources for dating castles are documents but their record is frequently incomplete and they need to be interpreted with regard to architectural detail and historical probability. Excavation will normally elucidate the building sequence but datable finds will be few; most early medieval pottery is not amenable to close dating. The problem is difficult for large castles but worse for the little mottes that often have no medieval record. Most of these were occupied by vassals of the border barons; and although they proliferated during the anarchy of Stephen's reign, 1134-54, most will be earlier. There was a pre-Conquest tradition of unlicensed castle building in Normandy itself, so it is likely that some here will go back to the early years of the Conquest.

Fig 49 Norman castles in the study area, plus Halton, Hen Domen, Montgomery, Knighton, Brecon and Cardiff (Hogg and King 1963, 1967 and 1970; and Ordnance maps for those east of the longitude of English Bicknor)

A Almeley	H Hopton	P Pembridge
B Brampton Bryan	He Herefordshire	R Richard's Castle
Br Bredwardine	Beacon	Ra Raglan
C Caerwent	K Kilpeck	S Shrawardine
D Dorstone	L Llancillo	Sk Skenfrith
Di Dinham	Ly Lyonshall	T Treago
E English Bicknor	M Madley	W Wigmore
Ea Eardisley	MC Mortimer's Cross	We Weobley
Ew Ewyas Harold	Mu Much Dewchurch	Wh White Castle
G Grosmont	N Newport, Gwent	

Plate 21 Richard's Castle motte

It is generally thought that the idea of the motte and bailey was brought here from the continent in the mid-eleventh century, although Davison thought the castle mound, the motte, might have been invented by the Normans after the invasion. Certainly early English castles were built both with and without mottes. The latter may have had timber towers, possibly close-boarded to resist penetration by firebrands. It would have been an obvious step to cover the lower part with turf for further protection, and even fill in the bottom with earth, thus creating a motte surmounted by a tower.

The occurrence of castles without mottes is of special significance for the investigation of our pre-Conquest castles. It had been thought that these would be recognizable as the earliest phases of the mottes at Richard's Castle, Ewyas Harold and Hereford. Curnow and Thompson showed, however, that the huge motte at Richard's Castle (pl 21) belongs to the twelfth-century castle. If the pre-Conquest castle of Auretone was on the same site as the fortifications of Richard FitzOsbern, it is beneath the stone keep on the motte.

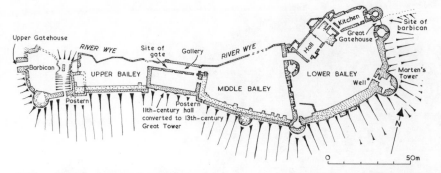

Fig 50 Plan of Chepstow Castle (After Ministry of Works Official Guide 1955). Crown Copyright - reproduced with permission of the Controller of Her Majesty's Stationery Ofice.

Chepstow is an early castle without a motte (fig 50). Built by William FitzOsbern probably between 1067 and 1070, it was described by Taylor as 'historically and architecturally one of the most important castles in the Welsh March'. Instead of a motte, the first castle had a stone hall, converted in the thirteenth century to a three storey tower. The hall is held to derive from the same ancestry as the one of 994, or a decade or two later, at Langeais on the Loire. Measuring thirty-two by twelve metres, it is the kind of building that may be present in other important castles. The thirteenth-century keep at Skenfrith is not on an earlier mound; it seems the eleventh century castle there also lacked a motte. Ludlow had no motte and was stone from the outset. The royal castle at Brockhurst, first recorded in 1154, was also stone-built from the start, without a motte.

The early castles would have been surrounded where necessary by a ditch to provide an internal bank to carry a palisade. A most spectacular example of such a ring-work is the summit Citadel within the Herefordshire Beacon hillfort, which yielded twelfth-century pottery. Some of the ditch spoil might also be thrown outwards to make a counterscarp bank as seen on the Bayeux tapestry round the castles at Dol, Dinan and Bayeux. The motte at Pontesbury probably started as a ring-work and had a stone tower added in the twelfth century. At Castell Bryn Amlwg a ring-work formed the first defence and a circular stone keep was added in the thirteenth century.

The earth motte offered a cheap alternative to the stone tower. Spoil from a circular ditch gave a flat-topped mound, about thirty-seven metres diameter, reducing to fifteen on top. It was sometimes built around a wooden tower; but tower posts may have been set in the

Plate 22   Hopton Castle tower house of about 1300

top of the mound, almost certainly so when renewal was needed. At Smethcott the tower post-holes came through the top of the motte.

The central hall, or the motte, was normally accompanied by a subsidiary enclosure, a bailey, for stables and workshops. Later, baileys were sometimes used for spacious residences. There might be more than one; in addition to an inner ward containing the hall, Chepstow had upper and lower baileys from the beginning, protected by their own curtain walls. At Kilpeck there are three outer enclosures as well as an inner bailey. Some of the little mottes in west Herefordshire and Shropshire, known locally as tumps and often labelled 'tumulus' on old maps, have no visible baileys.

The functions of the stone hall as residence and of the wooden tower as stronghold came to be combined in large rectangular keeps in the twelfth century. Good examples were built at Lydney, Goodrich, Monmouth and St. Briavels. From this developed the tower house, with entry on the ground floor, fireplaces and other refinements in the late thirteenth century: Clun and Hopton Castle (pl 22).

In the late eleventh century the French were experimenting with round towers and the vogue soon spread to Germany. It was possibly

German influence that brought the round keep to the southern Marches in the late twelfth or early thirteenth century. A fine example at Longtown is now dated later than 1200 (pl 23). Others survive at Caldicot, Lyonshall and Skenfrith and are also thought to have existed at Ashton in north Herefordshire, Caerleon, Llancillo and Monmouth. A few occur further north, for example at Castell Bryn Amlwg and Hawarden. Most of the circular form's advantages could be obtained by a multangular tower, like the octagonal one at Richard's Castle. Contemporary with central towers were many shell-keeps with minor towers incorporated in the curtain wall as at Wigmore. The rectangular wall towers of earlier times were increasingly supplanted by semicircular ones; and as the thirteenth century wore on the separate keep became less popular. More defenders manned the bailey wall in which elaborate gate-houses and extra large towers were built. The gate-houses at St Briavels and Llangibby became virtually self-contained fortresses. At Chepstow, Martin's Tower is like a secondary keep in the bailey wall. Barbicans, as at Goodrich, sometimes covered the approach to the drawbridge, with particularly long ones at Brampton Bryan and Abergavenny. In the outer bailey at Clifford twin circular towers project at the far end of the gate passage. With such devices and the provision of machicolations on towers and battlements the fourteenth century castle was nearly immune from attack.

The Welsh Marches as defined in this study hold some 260 castles in Hogg and King's list of pre-1215 sites and more than 90 later ones.

Castles west of the Wye

The Wye separated most of the English from the Welsh and important castles were built along it: at Clifford, Hay, Bredwardine, Hereford, Goodrich, English Bicknor, Monmouth, St Briavels and Chepstow. Standing on the Welsh or English side, according to local tactical or wider strategic requirements, they formed the Norman base line.

Clifford and Hay guarded the exit of the Wye from upland Wales, the sensitivity of the English here shown by a dozen or more undocumented mottes extending south-east to Dorstone in the Golden Valley. A string of mottes along that valley brings us close to another line from Madley to Much Dewchurch, placed as though to screen Hereford. More mottes in the upper Monnow valley show the fear of eruptions from the Black Mountains which might have threatened Hereford. The lower Monnow valley, the boundary of the Anglicized Welsh of Archenfield, was strongly occupied with castles at Monmouth, Grosmont, Skenfrith and White Castle. The last three were known as

Plate 23 Longtown Castle keep

the Three Castles and were long held by the Crown although garrisoned by various lords. They formed a triangle of power in a vital area. There are more mottes in central Gwent and still more on the coastal plain. There were early castles at Caldicot, Caerwent, Dinham, Newport and Caerleon.

The stone castles that were in use in the southern border in the mid thirteenth century indicate the resources committed to the defence of the southern March as a result of the campaign of Llewellyn the Great. Old sites were refortified and no fewer than ten new castles were built between Chepstow and Newport; Abergavenny, Usk, Caerleon and Newport remained occupied. This pattern persisted with little change until the mid fourteenth century, after which only Pembridge, in Welsh Newton parish, and Raglan were added.

Castles in the central Marches

There are few castles east of the line Hereford-Ludlow-Shrewsbury, save for a string along Corve Dale, the easy route into the Midlands. By contrast the plains of west Herefordshire are thick with undocumented mottes filling the space between early castles like Weobley, Eardisley, Huntington, Kington and Wigmore. The close cover extends north-westwards into Powys, creating a defensive zone sixteen kilometres wide. There are particularly dense groups of mottes around Almeley and Wigmore, where a castle had been built on ground that was waste before 1086. Wigmore was away from any east-west route and was presumably selected for land ownership rather than strategic reasons.

Some Shropshire motte groups look especially interesting. A line of five extends along the north-east front of the Long Mynd from Pontesbury. Another group around Bishop's Castle guarded against incursions from the upper Severn valley. A formidable cluster of tall, narrow-topped mottes is seen between Montgomery and Shrewbury. Observing that the farms on which they stand were held in recognition of castle guard duty at Montgomery, King and Spurgeon postulated farmstead fortification accompanying resettlement with soldier-farmers after Welsh raids. They should date between 1086, when the area was waste, and 1102, when the Earl of Shrewsbury held the Lordships of Montgomery and Chirbury, for most of them were held by the Corbets who were important tenants of the Earl. The mottes around Caus Castle, another Corbet possession, may have a similar origin. Apart from the presumed disuse of most mottes, the mid thirteenth-century pattern was little changed. Major sites rendered in stone included Lyonshall, Wigmore, Richard's Castle, Ludlow, Bishop's Castle and Caus. By the mid fourteenth century many were no longer defensible.

Castles of the northern Marches

North of the Severn, in less populated lands, there are fewer castles.

Between the river at Shrawardine and the Dee near Chirk a line of mottes forms a frontier to thwart access to the Shropshire lowlands. Their role was like that of the Mercian Wat's Dyke, just to the west of them. It was an area where the Welsh succeeded in retaking land in the twelfth century, including Oswestry and, south of the Severn, Caus. The many castles in east Shropshire, including Wem, Hodnet and Moreton Corbet, remained in use into the thirteenth and fourteenth centuries while unsettled conditions persisted.

In the far north most castles are along the Dee or west of it. The activity of early years was followed by abandonment. By 1350, between the Dee and the Clwyds only Flint, Hawarden and Holt were certainly occupied. More castles are securely documented at this time east of the Dee, at Chester, Shotwick, Frodsham, Beeston and Halton.

Late castle building

No major campaigns into Wales were undertaken after the suppression of Owen Glyndwr's rebellion in 1403, so most castles became redundant.

Plate 24   Raglan Castle, the Great Gate seen from the keep

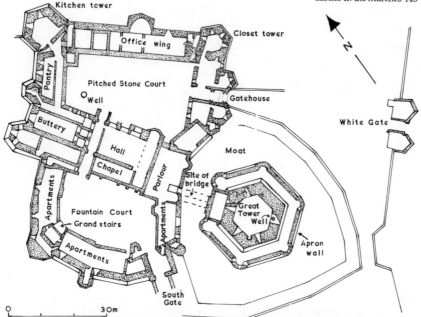

Fig 51 Ground floor plan of Raglan Castle (Somewhat simplified from Ministry of Works Official Guide Plan 1950). Crown Copyright - reproduced with permission of the Controller of Her Majesty's Stationery Office.

Furthermore, the devastation wreaked by the Welsh, coming on top of a general agrarian decline, left most landowners impoverished. They were more likely to sell part of their arable than add machicolations to the ancestral home. Moreover, the national trend was for more spacious and civilized residences. Those who could afford it left their draughty castles for new houses. Where castles were retained the windows were often enlarged and additional fireplaces built. Some continued in use into the seventeenth century but when recommissioned in the Civil War many were badly decayed. Stokesay, Brampton Bryan, Monmouth and Goodrich changed hands during that war and the fall of Raglan in 1646 signalled the effective end of Royalist resistance.

It was the improved fortunes of a small landowner, William ap Thomas, that had permitted a start on rebuilding Raglan Castle in the 1430s (fig 51). His son William Herbert, later Earl of Pembroke, amassed a wealth of lucrative lands and offices, particularly as a result of supporting Edward IV at the Battle of Mortimer's Cross in 1461. He undertook the building of the palatial stronghold seen today, a fortress offering comfort and security appropriate to royal visitors. His continental experience of the resurgent enthusiasm for keeps led to the

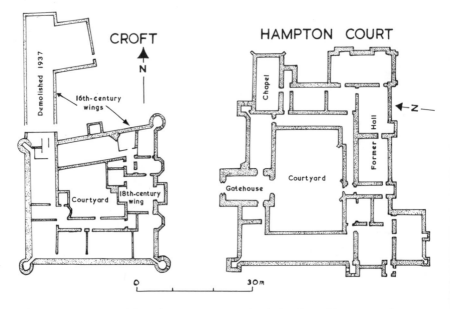

Fig 52 Two Herefordshire fortified houses: Croft Castle and Hampton Court. From Royal Commission on Historical Monuments (England) plans

building of a massive hexagonal one with its own apron wall and wet moat. This was outside the main castle enclosure, which was itself fortified with closely set multangular towers (pl 24). The only other major Welsh border castle to be reconstructed in the fifteenth century was Newport, rebuilt after devastation by Glyndwr's forces. Raglan was specially important.

Meanwhile less wealthy landowners built more modest fortified houses. The typical form of the finer examples was quadrangular with towers at the corners and suites of rooms about a central courtyard (fig 52). This is well shown at Treago Castle, only twenty-one metres square but having differently sized circular towers projecting far beyond this. Croft Castle similarly has circular towers projecting from the original courtyard plan which has sides thirty-four metres long; and Hampton Court, which received a licence to crenellate in 1435, is thirty nine metres square. The delapidated remains of a similar castle licensed in 1460 lie within a wet moat at Bronsil in Eastnor parish. Originally provided with corner, interval and gate towers, it shows a concern for impressive defence that is remarkable for a castle only fifty metres square.

CHAPTER TEN

Town and Country
In the Middle Ages

The royal castles and their baronial neighbours set the fashion in fortification, providing both strong-points of defence and garrisons to spearhead the assault against Wales. For the further supply of men and provisions the local area was called upon; settlement and castle came to be closely integrated (fig 53). Just as the motte was set beside church and manor farm, so was the larger castle associated with a town. At Hereford, Caerleon, Shrewsbury and Chester a castle was placed at the perimeter of the existing town which took on the plan and function of an extensive bailey. Hereford's medieval defences have been described (fig 47); its castle was rebuilt in stone and occupied into the later Middle Ages but was demolished in the quest for building stone for a growing city. At Shrewsbury too the medieval town defences took in the castle site (fig 55) but stone robbing and encroachment have largely eclipsed the mighty motte and bailey, seat of the Earl of Shrewsbury. At Chester a massive castle complex evolved on the banks of the Dee just outside the Roman fortress wall.

New boroughs were often founded to accompany new castles. Such 'plantation', with rectangular street grids, goes back to Saxon times but the Normans added castles. Beresford discussed English plantation towns in general and Noble discerned four phases of castle and borough establishment in the Marches between 1066 and 1250.

Within a few years of the Conquest, castles were built at Wigmore and Clifford, and the one at Ewyas Harold was rebuilt. These gave a base from which to assault Wales and boroughs were attached. The early castles at Chepstow and Monmouth may have had boroughs that escaped documentation. The town defences at Monmouth are Edwardian but the suburb of Over Monnow is protected by a defensive ditch, Clawdd Du, and has a Norman church. At Wigmore the borough was probably laid out parallel to the ridge on which the church stands and the first castle, without a motte, may have been nearer the church. The extra ground required for the later stone castle was found on the wider part of the ridge to the west. Wigmore borough only gave rise to a large village. Clifford and Ewyas Harold saw even less success. Their founder, William FitzOsbern, probably inherited the pre-Conquest castle borough at Richard's Castle, which was given a town bank in the thirteenth century but probably failed soon after.

Fig 53 Medieval boroughs in the Welsh Marches

A second phase of plantation, from the late eleventh to the late twelfth century, involved some of the lesser barons who were soon to be known as 'Lords Marcher'. The de Lacys added a castle to Anglo-Saxon Weobley, creating a borough with an irregular street plan, and possibly set out a new borough beside Grosmont castle. At White Castle there are hints of an unrecorded borough by the castle. The grid-iron of borough plantation is apparent at Trelleck village where there were 271 burgages in 1306; one hundred and two of them had been destroyed in 1295. The lay-out of Dorstone village and castle led Noble to suggest a possible borough there too. Early in the reign of Henry I a new honour was created for Adam de Port around Kington; his new borough should be centred around Castle Hill and Kington church.

The third phase saw the establishment of Huntington, probably between 1174 and 1190, but commerce preferred Kington; only the ghost of Huntington borough remains between castle and chapel. Hay, in Powys, was now laid out as a castle borough. On the Black Mountains, Longtown castle was being built between 1185 and 1195. Attached to it is a remarkably high bank, once thought to be Roman, enclosing 1.2 hectare; the borough lies to the south with its thirteenth-century chapel overlooking a triangular market place.

There were now enough castles but boroughs continued to be founded. In west Herefordshire licences were granted for markets and fairs at Eardisley in 1233 and Pembridge in 1240. Neither village saw much development. Ploughfield, described as a borough in 1273, is now only a hamlet in Preston-on-Wye parish. In east Herefordshire boroughs with no castles, but enjoying the patronage of the Bishop of Hereford or the Prior of Leominster, flourished at Bromyard, Ledbury, Ross and Leominster.

A similar pattern of plantations obtained in Shropshire. Ludlow, the finest, was founded by the de Lacys. On a site chosen for its defensive capability, the castle was integral with the town defences, though the early borough at Dinham is not thought to have extended as far as Mill Street. The enlarged grid-iron of the thirteenth-century town forms the modern street plan (fig 54).

Against Wales, new towns were planted to support castles at Clun, Bishop's Castle, Caus, Oswestry, Ellesmere and Wem, most achieving only moderate success. Caus had only nine of its thirty-three burgages in the outer bailey occupied in 1540; they have long since been abandoned. Among boroughs set up solely for commercial gain, success attended Newport, Market Drayton and Madeley. Less profitable were Baschurch, Ruyton-eleven-towns and Acton Burnell.

The coastal road to North Wales was barred by the Edwardian castle of Flint. The adjoining borough grid-iron was laid out on virgin

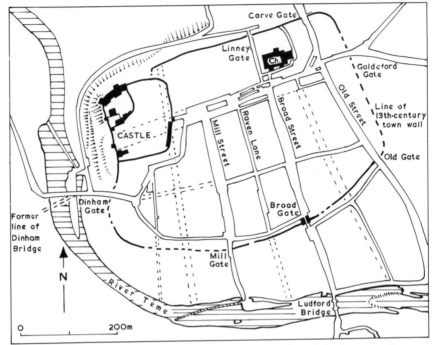

Fig 54 Plan of Ludlow showing the town wall with the original seven gates
and probable earlier streets as pecked lines

ground in 1277 and completed in less than five years using, amongst
others, carpenters from Derbyshire and ditch-diggers from Yorkshire,
brought thither under armed guard. Nine hundred and fifty ditch-
diggers were employed in the first week's work.

In the successful boroughs that became market towns there will
be ample material for the topographer and local historian; the oppor-
tunities for economic excavation will always be few. It is in boroughs
that were still-born or fell into disuse prematurely that the archaeologist could most profitably be employed.

Later town defences

In the successful boroughs the defences had to be refurbished and
extended. Eighteenth-century cartographers have often left us with
detailed plans of town walls, gates and bastions but only by excavation
and sympathetic development can this part of our urban legacy be
revealed to the public. This happened in Hereford, where parts of the

thirteenth-century wall and bastions can now be seen. Several border towns share the same history of refortification in stone following earlier earth and timber defences. At Chepstow the Port Wall across the promontory that holds the town and castle was built between 1272 and 1278; it was fronted by a ditch six metres wide and only a metre deep. Seven of the ten semicircular towers survive and there is one rectangular tower resembling that at Hereford in Blue School Street which was rebuilt in that form during the Civil War.

Abergavenny's town defences are now virtually obliterated but their history is indicated by murage grants of 1241-6, 1259-64, 1295-1301 and 1314-19 which allowed the town to levy taxes or tolls to pay for them. A bank discovered in Castle Street is thought to date around 1250; a stone wall was added later. As at Hereford the defences were dilapidated by the time of the Civil War when the ditch was recut.

The earliest defences revealed at Shrewsbury date from about 1220-1242 (fig 55). At the top of the slope inside the Severn's meander, they are followed by the curving perimeter road between the Welsh and English bridges. The half-moon of the lower town defences was linked to the castle, commanding the neck of the meander, along the river-cliff top, though the line is only partly known. The castle was derelict by 1443 but in the Civil War the defences were refurbished and in 1645 on Cromwell's orders the riverside district of Smithfield was protected by a new wall from Gilbert's Tower to the Welsh Bridge.

At Chester the medieval wall followed the Roman fortress walls on the north and east but extended to the Dee to south and west (fig 31). The medieval castle was placed in the south-west corner of the fifty-three-hectare enclosure. No gate survives but some wall towers and the north-west Spur, built in 1322, are still visible.

Moated sites

Probably throughout the period of castle and town fortification the smaller landowners were protecting themselves and their property by building strong houses or digging moats. More than seventy moats are visible in both Shropshire and Herefordshire (fig 56). Extant ones are few in north-west Cheshire and rare in Gwent and Clwyd, as in the rest of Wales. Their frequency in the border does not necessarily reflect the proximity of Wales, for wet moats are even more common in Suffolk and Warwickshire. Although useless against an army, they would have been a deterrent to robbers and vagrants. They could be stocked with fish and would keep the house-site dry. The English distribution may reflect geology, since digging in rock was expensive, but it is more

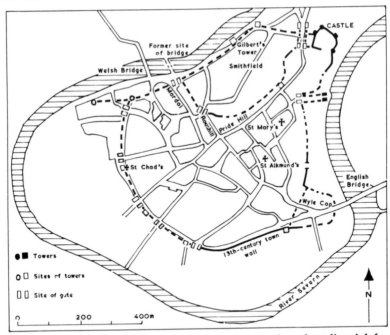

Fig 55 Plan of Shrewsbury showing modern roads and medieval defences
(Based on Carver and Wills 1974, p 182 and Carver 1974, fig 28)

likely to mirror different social conditions either side of the frontier.
Most moats, in the Midlands at least, seem to be earlier than 1350, with
few likely to be dug after 1500. The bridge timber of Shackerley Mound
had a tree-ring date of about 1289. Although the Warwickshire moats
are commonly in areas of late woodland clearance, the generalization
does not seem applicable to the Marches. Here it illustrates the
increasing separation of manor from village.

Moats are usually about ten metres wide, enclosing rectangles
with sides thirty to fifty metres long; though Wormbridge Priory
Grange at Uppington encloses 1.5 hectare. Needing water, most are on
the bottom clay lands or beside streams. There are few lowland
parishes in Herefordshire and Shropshire that do not have one and
some have two or three since not only manor houses but granges and
hunting lodges could be moated. In low-lying areas they provided dry
sites for haystacks. Cheshire has about 200 moats, of 0.1-0.6 hectare,
many known only from crop marks. In Shropshire, the total from all
sources is over 150.

At Hen Gwrt, Gwent, the fourteenth-century moat was abandoned
in the fifteenth, but re-occupied in the sixteenth as the lodge of Raglan

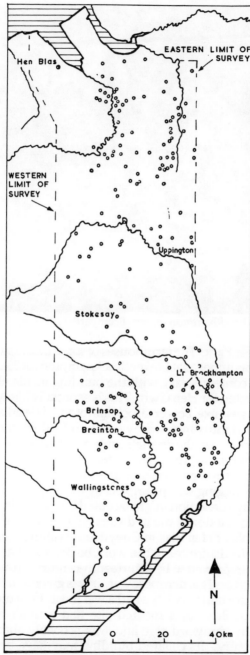

Fig 56 Major moated sites in the Marches

Plate 25 Lower Brockhampton manor, Bromyard

Castle Red Deer Park. The farmhouses of some moats survive: in stone as at Brinsop or timber as at Lower Brockhampton (pl 25). Although the moat may be contemporary with the building inside, it will often be later, as suggested for Hen Gwrt. This is especially likely in existing or deserted villages, like Lower Brockhampton. The adjacent Norman chapel ruin and indistinct nearby earthworks there indicate a larger settlement, earlier than the fine half-timbered fourteenth-century house; but the moat is crossed through a fifteenth-century timber gatehouse and this may be the structure that dates the moat.

If moat-digging was prompted by the dispersal of village communities, village desertion might be dated by excavating the moat. No more than about a dozen moated sites have been investigated in the border and only at Hen Blas in Clwyd and Wallingstones, Tre-Essey, in south Herefordshire could the work be described as extensive.

Wallingstones proved to be a thirteenth-century strong house, a hall with undercroft and garderobe tower. It was given a curtain wall in the fifteenth century and may have had a wet moat. On a bluff by the Wye near Hereford, Breinton's moated site had a small ditch and low rampart on the landward side and was probably abandoned in the thirteenth century. Its cellared building may have been simply the vicarage for the neighbouring church about which are the earthworks of a deserted village. At Hen Blas, near Flint, a twelfth-century motte site was in domestic use in the thirteenth and fourteenth centuries.

To rebuild such sites in the mind, existing farms and houses may serve as models; places like Lower Brockhampton or Stokesay Castle. At Stokesay the late thirteenth-century hall, flanked by towers, occupied the west side of a courtyard now entered through an Elizabethan gatehouse. It is much closer to the castle model; and closer still is the contemporary fortified house at Acton Burnell, a keep-like residence with towers at each corner.

Ecclesiastical sites

While the king and his barons built their castles and the second-tier landlords dug their moats, the clergy were busy drawing in money as gifts and tithes to build and rebuild churches and establish abbeys and nunneries with extensive estates. In 1066 there were some thirty-one major religious establishments in the border, the English minsters and the equivalent Welsh 'clas' churches. These were scattered as the accident of benefactor or patron saint dictated. There were only two in Gwent east of the Usk, at Caerwent and Llandogo, whereas in Archenfield there were five, reflecting the activity of St Dubricius and others: Dewchurch, Garway, Hentland, Moccas and Welsh Bicknor. There was none in the Welsh areas of the northern border.

Seven of the English minster churches were in the towns of Bromyard, Chester, Hereford, Ledbury, Leominster and Monmouth. Those at Bromfield and Stanton Lacy were near Ludlow and others at Withington and Moreton six kilometres from Hereford. Few were far from rich farming areas and none was remote.

The Normans established more lowland monasteries, including St Kynemark's Priory Chepstow, Flanesford Priory Goodrich, Dore Abbey, Grey Friars and Black Friars Hereford, Leominster Priory, Wigmore Abbey, Chirbury and Alberbury Priories, Wombridge Priory and St Mary's Vale Royal. The Cistercians and others looked to remote woodlands and mountain valleys for their sites. First among them is Tintern Abbey, founded in 1131, mostly rebuilt in the thirteenth century and still magnificently ruinous in the Wye gorge, though dissolved in 1536. By contrast the thirteenth-century Grace Dieu Abbey, Llantilio Crossenny has disappeared. In the high valleys of the Black Mountains are Llanthony Abbey (pl 26) and Craswall Priory; in the hills west of Wigmore there were houses of nuns and monks at Limebrook. At the entrance to the Severn gorge Buildwas Abbey (pl 27) was built about 1148 on a narrow plain bordered by steep wooded hills, like Tintern.

Plate 26   Llanthony Priory, built between 1175 and 1230;
the nave from the south chapels

Many of these monasteries were enormous. Although the church was the dominating architectural feature, the cloisters and kitchens, guesthouses and stables, workshops and farm buildings extended far. The exposed walls alone of Tintern Abbey cover about 1.7 hectare. Early antiquaries exposed many foundations but left much unaccounted for and did little to pursue the sequence of building and repair. The formidable task of determining the full extent and history of such monasteries continues, notably on sites like Tintern and Haughmond that are in the care of the State.

Henry VIII's dissolution of the monasteries meant that most of them became simply quarries for stone. No such fate befell the parish churches and cathedrals which therefore offer a wealth of extant

Plate 27   Buildwas Abbey, built 1135-1200; the nave from the west

architectural and documentary evidence for the post-Conquest period. Through them we can see how European culture, as expressed in stone and religion, could be disseminated through the medium of powerful, wealthy landlords. Especially noteworthy are the twelfth-century carvings of the 'Herefordshire School' which was responsible for the decoration of several churches in Herefordshire and neighbouring English counties. Their work, most magnificently displayed on the little church at Kilpeck, drew its motifs from Anglo-Saxon, Continental, Celtic and Viking art.

As more churches have become redundant there has been an increase in detailed recording and some excavation about them but the location of lost churches remains an important objective for the field archaeologist. Redundancy has a long, if intermittent, history in the border. In north Herefordshire, when the churches of Great and Little Collington were united in 1352, Little Collington was retained for its greater convenience of access and better repair; but where was Great Collington? - probably not far from the modern church, built to replace Little Collington a kilometre to the north-west.

In 1364 the nearby churches of Whyle and Pudlestone were united and there is now no church at Whyle. Such unions, the result perhaps of a local epidemic in small parishes over-endowed with churches, and a re-distribution of population, reflected adjustment to a new economic balance. Other churches suffered from war. In 1406 some twenty-six churches in Herefordshire were exempted from contributing to the King's Aid because they had been 'destroyed'. In fact only Bacton, Hentland and St Weonard's in that list exhibit architectural evidence of large-scale rebuilding in the fifteenth or early sixteenth century.

Several churches were abandoned in the nineteenth century and rebuilt at more convenient locations, including Collington 1856, Llanwarne 1864 and Little Marcle 1870.

There are many more lost chapels, though some would have been no more than special rooms in large houses. The chapel at Webton near Madley was recorded in the Bishop's Registers in 1536 but was in ruins when Taylor mapped Herefordshire in 1786. He shows another chapel in the same parish at Wisteston, and a ruin at Hampton Wafer, possibly the chapel listed in 1536. Old chapel ruins are marked on the deserted village site at Newton, Clifford where a fine motte and bailey is the obvious landmark today; and so are Vowmynd chapel ruins at Mynydd Brith, Dorstone, and those of St Ailworth's Walterstone, Coughton near Ross, Glewstone in Llangarron, Glynstone in Llangrove, St Wolstan's in Welsh Newton and Trewadoc in Garway. To these may be added St Dubricius' chapel in Woolhope and Hardwick Chapel, Kenderchurch, mentioned about 1300 in a cartulary of Ewyas Harold Priory. The incidence of lost chapels is far greater in Shropshire; Duke recorded 105 in 1844.

Villages and homesteads

The Marches today exhibits a mixture of villages, hamlets, isolated farms and outlying cottages. The emphasis on dispersal was long interpreted as a legacy from a Celtic pattern but it is now recognized that most of the dispersed elements are later than 1086. The historical evidence for this view in part of Shropshire has been set out in Volume VIII of the Victoria County History for that county. A valuable archaeological insight into migration within parishes since Anglo-Saxon times has been given by Wade-Martin's East Anglian studies. The gradual shift there from old to new focuses is in marked contrast to the familiar processes of the Midlands and Yorkshire. In those areas villages often disappeared suddenly following seventeenth-century sheep enclosure, or were dispersed equally rapidly by later parliamentary enclosures. In either case, by the time the village was abandoned or stripped of its main farms, its population was large and so too was its mark on the landscape: deeply hollowed streets and upstanding house platforms, often accompanied by a lonely church. Desertion usually meant depopulation and was late enough to be verified in national tax returns.

The search for deserted village sites in the Welsh Marches is difficult. Hamlets are widespread and did not attract the ancillary settlement that may sustain a nucleated village through hard times. Secondly, although it is recognized that open-field agriculture was common in both English and Welsh areas, most land on the border was enclosed early, while settlements were still small enough to be covered by the barns of a modern farm: over 80% of Shropshire for example was enclosed by 1675. Thirdly, such enclosure was probably accompanied by migration within the parish rather than out of it. As a result there are few border sites comparable with the classic desertions of Warwickshire. Interest focuses on shrunken sites and often the same term 'deserted village' is used of shrunken villages or hamlets with gaps in their street frontage.

Hamlets are especially common in parts of Cheshire, west Shropshire, south Herefordshire and the Welsh counties, where they are often a Celtic legacy. Many were recorded as Welshries in Domesday Book, and their use of open-field agriculture is illustrated by ridge and furrow at Braggington and at Old Marton, the vill of Merton from which the Welsh inhabitants were evicted for joining the 1280 revolt. Some manors had more than one settlement, even in the time of Edward the Confessor. Many were waste in 1086, especially in the west.

Rowley's study of Corve Dale and the Clee hills showed that large numbers of medieval hamlets are now represented by a farm, a church or a few cottages. In the absence of maps or detailed terriers it is not possible to be certain that the medieval population figures refer to the location now bearing the name. Many have earthworks indicative of more extensive settlement but three-quarters are without earthworks or are occupied by modern buildings probably covering medieval houses.

Some of the possible oscillations of settlement history are shown at Abdon on the north side of Brown Clee Hill. About 1.3 hectare of irregular earthworks lies between the isolated church and the surviving farms and cottages. Late medieval decline is indicated from records and a long-house site excavated near the church yielded no finds later than about 1300. Another house site about 135 metres away was occupied by the sixteenth century when mining and quarrying became important locally; but the village was in decline again by the end of the eighteenth century.

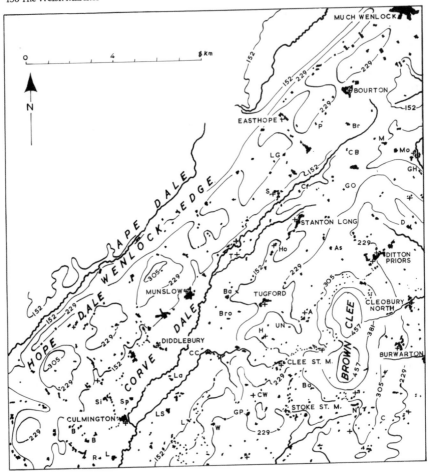

Fig 57 Corve Dale settlement (Source: Rowley 1972) Buildings shaded. Shrunken or deserted settlements shown by initial letters. Contours in metres.

A Abdon	CB Corve Barn	M Monk Hall
As Ashfield	D Derrington	Mo Monkhopton
B Bache	GH Gt Hudwick	N Newton
Ba Baucott	Go Gt Oxenbold	P Patton
Bo Bockleton Ct	GP Greater Poston	R Ruckley
Br Bradley	H Heath	S Shipton
Bro Broncroft	Ho Holdgate	Si Siefton
Bu Burley	L Langley	Sp Sparchford
C Coldgreen	LG Larden Grange	T Thonglands
CW Cold Weston	La Lawton	UN Upper Norncott
CC Corfham Castle	LS Little Sutton	W Witchcot
Cf Corfield	Ly Lydehole	

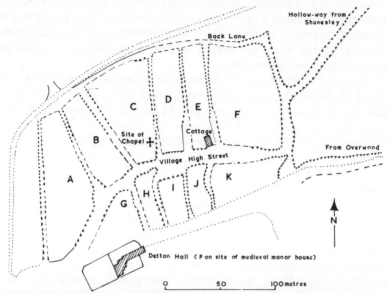

Fig 58 Detton Hall, the crofts (A-K) of the medieval village shown by earthworks before being levelled in 1960 (Stanford 1965, fig 16)

Abdon is at 247 metres, high up on marginal land, and it is possible that climatic deterioration or soil exhaustion encouraged its fourteenth-century desertion. This might also have been the case with other Brown Clee Hill sites like Heath and Cold Weston, both at about 244 metres and possessing extensive village earthworks. Like Abdon, Heath has an isolated chapel and Cold Weston a lonely church. Heath's earthworks seem to require more than the seven families assessed for tax in 1327 and point to the difficulty of relating earthworks to records when the components of the earthworks are not individually dated. Cold Weston was virtually deserted by 1341.

At Detton Hall, just east of the Clee Hills, a large field known as Chapel Field once contained hollow ways and platforms (fig 58). Excavation failed to produce structural evidence for any medieval buildings, which were presumably constructed in timber and laid without stone sills on the old ground surface. Pottery showed the site to have been abandoned around 1300. At its maximum extent there were probably, in addition to the manor house, at least two other large farms occuying the wide crofts F and K at the east end of the village street. The chapel, of which traces remained in the nineteenth century, held a central position and there were half a dozen narrower crofts, presumably the property of cottagers. The whole settlement may have held forty or fifty people. This may be compared with a total Domesday Book record of seven serfs, one villein, four bordars, and one 'radman', probably a free man. Multiplying by 3.5 to obtain total Domesday population, we arrive at forty-five persons, within the estimate based on earthworks.

Detton Hall and nearby Sidbury, a severely shrunken site, are both at 152 metres but similar sites occur even lower, down to Corfham Castle on the bank of the Corve at 125 metres. Factors other than climatic deterioration must be involved. These will include early enclosure of common fields and consolidation of holdings with new farms away from the old nucleus. Some farms will have increased at the expense of others and increased dispersal could result from waste-land squatter settlement.

At Hampton Wafer, in north-east Herefordshire, there is today only a single farm but in the early nineteenth century the ruins of what may have been the chapel existed nearby. Deeply eroded hollow ways between house platforms and a pond that proved to be a flooded stockyard suggested that the settlement was about the size of Detton. The pottery ranged from the eleventh century until about the time that the manor is known to have passed to the FitzAllens of Hampton Court, in 1330. Most of their resources went into the latter manor and the consequent neglect of Hampton Wafer may have encouraged enclosure and transfer of population to new outlying farms. There is no recorded evidence of these being earlier than the seventeenth century so there may have been a hiatus betweeen the desertion and the establishment of the dispersed pattern two centuries or more later. The problem is not confined to Hampton Wafer; we should not overlook the susceptibility of hamlets to epidemics and possible reduction by plague. Between Hampton Wafer and Detton Hall the churches of the two Collingtons were united in 1352, and those of Whyle and Pudleston in 1364, both on the petition that plague had depopulated the area.

Both Runston and St Brides Netherwent in Gwent have isolated chapels beside village earthworks. After a long period of decline from the Middle Ages, Runston's eight house sites were abandoned between 1772 and 1800. At St Brides ten possible house sites have been located. Near Hereford the village of Stretton Sugwas contained eleven cottages as late as 1757. Now there are none. When the church was pulled down in 1877 and the new one built a kilometre away, only Court Farm was left. East of the Lugg at Preston Wynne the church stands alone beside a large field corrugated by the hollow ways of a deserted settlement.

The voluntary or enforced removal of labourers from the neighbourhood of the manor farm led frequently to straggling unplanned settlements on waste hillside or forest edge, or near the parish boundary in waste beyond the common fields. Occupied by the least well organized members of the community, they were particularly vulnerable in times of rural depression and many were abandoned or severely depleted earlier this century. The earthworks of such an abandoned forest-edge hamlet may be seen on Garnons Hill, Bishopstone, where ten houses stood in 1886. There may have been a double desertion: from Bishopstone to Garnons Hill and then to extra-parochial destinations. The reorganization of labourers' accommodation for the benefit of the owners of the great hall is thought to have been behind the abandonment of Braggington on the Shropshire-Powys border. The hamlet had probably been established in waste land after the Norman Conquest and excavation of a house site within an extensive moated area, showed that it had been abandoned in the seventeenth century, possibly when Braggington Hall was erected nearby in 1675. At Pitchford, south of Shrewsbury, there was formerly a village on the ground below the hall, near the church. The hall was built about 1560-70 and the village was possibly moved then to the main road. At Morville, east Shropshire, the village centre was cleared for landscaping in the sixteenth century; but the inhabitants may only have gone to the village edge.

Moran's study of the removal and re-erection of both timber-framed and stone houses in the Shropshire parish of Myddle in the seventeenth century makes such moves appear a little less onerous. It may also explain why the traces of houses on deserted sites can be so fugitive; why, for example, so few tilestones await recovery. At Hampton Wafer the very footings of the walls had been removed.

Gaps in some villages will have been occasioned when people moved to industrial sites at the edge of the parish or on marginal land elsewhere. Such would have been the potteries, charcoal burning sites, brick and lime kilns, quarries and mines. With the decline of such industries in the last century, hundreds of house sites and paddocks have been deserted. At Hangstree Gate, Willey, a sixteenth-century map showed a sizeable hamlet, presumably the home of iron-workers, but there are no houses there now.

Apart from the widespread examples of village or hamlet desertion it must be remembered that there is probably no settlement that does not exhibit house platforms that are unoccupied and hollow ways that lead nowhere. To this extent almost every Welsh border village is a shrunken settlement. The seeds of dispersal may have been there before the Conquest but the construction of castles and moated establishments accelerated the process of community fragmentation which continued for a variety of reasons.

CHAPTER ELEVEN

The Archaeology of Rural Industries

The post-medieval development of an increasingly literate and central-ized state has given the historian masses of documents from which to reconstruct the recent past; but there remain small unlit areas where archaeological techniques still contribute. 'Industrial Archaeology' is primarily the province of the economic historian, historical geographer and engineer and in many of its enquiries the archaeological input will be small. These are areas where industry has persisted into the era of detailed Ordnance Survey maps and where the relics are abundant and often conspicuous: regions like the Forest of Dean, the Shelve district, Coalbrookdale and the Clwyd coalfield. Nor are specifically archaeo-logical techniques likely to provide the major contribution to the study of post-medieval transport, to the tramways, canals, railways and roads.

Welsh Marches industry (fig 59) has always taken place in a rural setting, even since the Industrial Revolution, but the activities that are our concern here are further distinguished by their dispersal and small-scale; so that in decline their remains have slipped easily into grass-grown mounds and merged with the agricultural scene.

Before the steam age, the need to derive power from water and fuel from wood, as charcoal, were common locating factors for indus-try. The ungraded character of most border streams ensured an adequacy of breaks in profile for siting water mills and, particularly south of the middle Severn, the steep-sided, narrow tributary valleys were readily dammed for mill-ponds.

In Herefordshire there were ninety-two mills in 1086, while Taylor's map of 1786 showed 209 mills and two former mills widely distributed on all the county's streams. In 1835 Bryant showed only 186 working mills and sixteen former sites. Today a recognizable mill is a rarity and an intact one, like the paper mill at Mortimer's Cross, a scheduled ancient monument. Mill sites had a long life. Excavated finds from Troy Mill on the Trothy, Gwent, ranged from the fourteenth to the eighteenth century. At Welsh Newton twelfth-century pottery came from the earliest part of the mill which was finally destroyed about 1700. Lower down the Mally Brook the mill at Dixton spanned the period 1200 to 1650.

In connection with the upstream works of water-mills it will be remembered that leats and weirs were also constructed to irrigate pastures. A famous set of such works was constructed by Rowland

Vaughan in the early seventeenth century at Turnastone in the Golden Valley of south-west Herefordshire. A Trench Royal was dug along the far side of the valley from the river, three metres wide and 1.2 metres deep; it was to be five kilometres long and could be used for transport on the farm; a smaller 'topping' trench was dug alongside the river. With the aid of sluices some 121 hectares of meadow could receive the muddy flood waters of winter, be watered again in April if need be, and be drowned once more two or three days before mowing. Flooding could also be used to clear snow from the meadows.

Much marginal land was coppiced to provide the small wood favoured by the charcoal burners and the stools of oak and ash often betray such management. On steep slopes circular terraces would be excavated about ten metres in diameter to take the wood stack for firing. Their inhospitable locations, indifferent of aspect and slope, usually makes confusion with hut terraces unlikely; black soil in their mole-hills often confirms their function. Charcoal burning must go back to prehistoric times; it continued as late as 1963 on Credenhill.

Most intensive charcoal-burning sites were probably related to a local iron-working, lime-burning or pottery kiln demand, so the terraces are often accompanied at no great distance by the earthworks and scars of such industries. Most frequent are the hollow ways scored on the hillside by iron-rimmed cart-wheels, connecting the terraces with the quarries and forges. A complex of such tracks, limestone quarries and charcoal-burning terraces, probably associated with the production of burnt lime for agriculture, may be seen below Croft Ambrey on Leinthall Earls Common.

Lime kilns are widespread. One in a large quarry in the Fishpool Valley at Croft would have served the needs of the castle estate. Above Leintwardine a fine range of three, with interconnecting stone chambers, also stands in a big quarry. On the dip-slope of Wenlock Edge bulldozers once broke into lost kilns above Siefton Forest Farm. Similar relics are to be found on all the major limestone outcrops; and also along thinner bands like the Psammosteus Limestone which outcrops on the upper slopes of many Herefordshire hills. Like the large sewers of major houses and abbeys, the kilns are frequently reported as caves, tombs and escape tunnels.

Potters too have made heavy demands on the forest, although we have little knowledge of their industry until after the Middle Ages. However, fourteenth /fifteenth-century wasters of jugs, storage vessels and ridge tiles were found at Ewloe, Clwyd in an area used by later potters. This may point towards continuity and encourage the search for medieval pottery sites in the vicinity of known post-medieval kilns. The earliest of the latter yet indicated in that part of Clwyd is at Buckley

KEY :- Navigable river
Canal
Tramway

where three waster pits date to the mid or late seventeenth century.

An important group of kiln sites of roughly this date is known in north-west Herefordshire with six in an area of twenty square kilometres, mostly in the ancient royal forest of Deerfold. Their depredations caused the warden to be charged with permitting their activity for his personal gain from the sale of firewood to the tune of forty pounds over the previous five years. Similar pottery has been found on other Herefordshire kiln sites at St Margarets, Whitney-on-Wye and Upton Bishop. There were potteries of the same period at Abergavenny, Gwehelog near Usk and Cwmcarvan south-west of Monmouth. Such potteries faded as mass-produced Staffordshire slipware came in around 1700.

The bed of a glass furnace was found at Glasshouse Farm, St Weonards, probably built by Lorrainers around 1600 to produce drinking glasses, window glass and linen smoothers. Since such furnaces were only the size of a large bread oven their discovery depends on the re-appearance of wasters as happened during bulldozing at Ruyton Park on fields named Glasshouse Bank on a survey of 1771. Both sites would have been used for less than fifty years since Lorrainers did not begin to settle in England until 1567 and in 1615 the use of timber as fuel for this purpose was banned. Some time after 1616 a coal-fired glasshouse was built by Mansell at Newnham-on-Severn where early seventeenth-century glass may be seen in house walls; but most glassmakers concentrated on the coalfield around Stourbridge where there were also refractory clays for crucibles.

Fig 59 Navigations, tramways and some early rural industrial sites.
f Iron forge/furnace g Glass furnace k Lime kiln p Pottery

C Coalbrookdale	MC Mortimer's	Wi Withington
E Elmbridge	Cross	WV Whitchurch Vagas
G Gunns Mills	W Wombridge	WW Wrockwardine Wood

Canals bac Brecon and Abergavenny
bc Birmingham
bljc Birmingham and Liverpool
    Junction
cc Chester
ec Ellesmere
hgc Herefordshire and Gloucestershire
kc Ketley

lc Leominster
mgc Montgomeryshire
moc Monmouthshire
sc Shropshire
swc Staffordshire and
    Worcestershire
syc Shrewsbury
tmc Trent and Mersey

Iron-working required water for washing the ore and water power for the furnace bellows and forge hammers. The hillside charcoal burners' terraces will therefore be at some distance from the streamside forge or furnace. In the Forest of Dean the combination of the Crease Limestone haematite and uncultivable terrain fit only for woodland made iron-working important. To produce one tonne of iron could require as much as a tonne and a half of charcoal, so the industry quickly spread beyond the ore outcrop and the limits of the Forest. Such dispersal had ancient precedents. At Whitchurch Vagas and Monmouth, Roman and medieval iron slags have been found near the sites of modern ironworks; and medieval iron-working went on at Trelleck and several other sites in that area. As well as Whitchurch there were eighteenth-century blast furnaces on tributaries of the Wye at Tintern, Redbrook, Lydbrook, Bishopswood and St Weonards, while the Forest was flanked on east and south by furnaces at Elmbridge, Gunns Mills, Flaxley, Blakeney and Lydney. The first commercially successful blast furnace in the area, at Lydbrook, was operated by William Herbert, Earl of Pembroke, in 1608. In the eighteenth century the Foleys held the major part of the industry hereabouts. What may have been one of their furnaces was excavated at Coed Ithel just north of Tintern. Probably built about 1650, it was stone-lined and conical with a pyramid top. Measuring 7.3 metres square, it would have been about six metres high, with a capacity of about twelve cubic metres. Forging of the iron often took place far away from the furnaces, as at Carey Mill and New Weir on the Wye, and at Llancillo, Peterchurch and Upleadon where water power and charcoal were assured. The charcoal furnaces and forges mostly failed before the end of the eighteenth century against the competition of coke-fired plant but their names survived, if only as 'Old Forge' or 'Old Furnace', to nineteenth-century maps.

In the Angidy valley at Tintern, where Britain's first water-powered wire-drawing works were built in 1566, there were twenty water-wheels in use by 1821. Today the ponds are the main evidence for the works that were only closed in 1901.

Just as the Dean iron industry extended into the quiet dingles of south Herefordshire and Gwent, the ramifications of Coalbrookdale reached into the valleys of the central Marches. The earlier introduction of the blast furnace there demanded extra charcoal before the adoption of coke allowed reconcentration around Coalbrookdale. A furnace was built at Cleobury Mortimer about the same time as that at Shifnal, 1562. It was one of a small group of ironworks on the Clee and Rea Brooks that used Clee Hill ore. Their heyday was in the eighteenth century but their origins may have been in the seventeenth. There were two forges at Cleobury Mortimer and two more five kilometres upstream at Prescott and Hardwick. On the Clee Brook at Charlcotte, another six kilometres north, the Cinder Hill Farm furnace is well preserved, built of stone, six metres square and 7.3 metres high, with the foundations of a store-house and large mounds of slag nearby. Most of the pig-iron from Charlcotte went to Bringewood, Bewdley and Stourport forges but transport difficulties and the competition of coke-iron led to decline in the late eighteenth century. There is no evidence that Charlcotte was working after 1792.

Charlcotte's furnace was first mentioned in 1712 when the manor was acquired by Richard Knight, ironmaster, of Bringewood, where an interesting early industrial complex was built in the wooded gorge where the Teme spills out of the Vale of Wigmore. Relics of this pioneering period include an eighteenth-century bridge over the Teme, a fine horse-shoe weir, and the remains of the wharf and tin-plating works. A famous collection of cast-iron tomb covers from Bringewood is at nearby Burrington Church (pl 28).

North of Coalbrookdale there were early furnaces at Wrockwardine and Wombridge; and the Tern valley had seven of Shropshire's fifteen forges in 1717. At least five large works operated in the fourteen kilometres between Moreton Corbet and the Severn, making 800-900 tonnes of wrought iron per annum. Moreton Corbet was probably working by 1666 and continued till the late eighteenth century. Wytheford Forge, with its dam, pool and watercourse system, is documented over the same period and there was a forge at Withington. Upton forge was established about 1675 and continued until about 1820; its waterworks originate at Duncote and extend for three kilometres. There had been a mill by Attingham Hall since the thirteenth century and in 1710 the Tern Forge was set up with three kilometres of waterworks upstream, including a pool, weirs, locks and wharfs. It closed in 1757.

With Abraham Darby's successful smelting of iron with coke instead of charcoal at Coalbrookdale in 1709 it was inevitable that coal would become the major locating factor for the iron industry, and this was confirmed when the steam engine removed the need for water power. The countryside furnaces and forges, hampered by transport costs, fell into second place behind the ironmasters of Coalbrookdale. There may be seen the foundations of the furnace built in 1638, in which the important smelt of 1709 took place. A second furnace was built there in 1715; others followed at Horsehay and Ketley between 1753 and 1756. As work concentrated in the gorge and on the hills of either bank Coalbrookdale hauled the world into new approaches to construction and transport. The first cast-iron wagon wheels were made in 1767.

Ten years later a huge iron beam inscribed ABRAHAM DARBY 1777 was cast for the rebuilding of the Old Furnace to help meet the requirements of the world's first iron bridge, started that year and opened on 1 January 1781. Magnificently arched over the Severn, its single span integrated the resources in minerals and personnel of both banks while permitting river traffic to proceed unhindered. With its main ribs weighing 5.8 tonnes each, and a total of 384.6 tonnes of iron in all, it was more than a technological triumph; it symbolized a new era as Industrial Man stepped along the road to new conceptions in communication. The world's first iron boat, The Trial, was built in

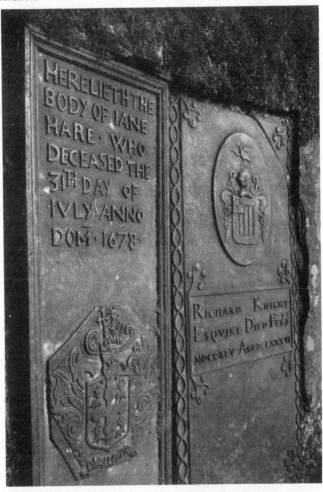

Plate 28   Iron tomb covers at Burrington church

1787 for use on the Severn. In 1788 the Ketley canal was completed, incorporating the first successful inclined plane in Britain, to lower the boats twenty-two metres to the ironworks. By 1793 the Hay incline, dropping sixty-three metres to the Severn, and the Windmill Hill incline to the north, were in use taking the Shropshire Canal to Coalport. In 1796 a trough of cast iron, made at Ketley, was used to carry the Shrewsbury Canal over the Tern at Longdon.

Meanwhile the completion of the Staffordshire and Worcestershire Canal and its junction with the Birmingham Canal in 1772 had linked the Trent and Severn; and by 1777 the Midlands network had an outlet to the Mersey. By the canal basin at the Severn terminus of the system the new town of Stourport came into being.

On the south-west border of the Marches the industrial archaeologist may navigate the restored Brecon and Abergavenny Canal with its 343-metre tunnel at Ashford, stone aqueduct over the Usk, locks and winding holes and variety of bridges of which there were formerly over a hundred in the fifty-three kilometres of restored canal. Work had started on this, as the Monmouthshire Canal, in 1792. By the beginning of the nineteenth century it had a number of tramway feeders bringing iron, coal and limestone to its wharfs. Such tramways, their wagons pulled by horses, often replaced failed canal schemes, as between Hereford and Brecon, and between Hay and Kington. Their courses may still be traced, albeit intermittently.

A canal was started in 1793 from Gloucester to Hereford. By way of the Oxenhall tunnel it reached Ledbury in 1798. The price of coal there fell from 24/- to 13/6; but no more was done until 1839 when the extension to Hereford was started. Before this was completed in 1845 the company was already thinking of selling out to the railway; and the Great Western Railway eventually acquired it. Many relics survive along its course and parts are currently being restored. South of the Oxenhall tunnel 'Lock Cottage' stands beside a series of four locks, and the entrances to the Ashperton and Aylestone Hill tunnels, 366 and 402 metres long respectively, may still be seen; but the long Frome embankment has been largely removed in recent years.

In 1777 Robert Whitworth was appointed to survey three canal schemes: Leominster to Stourport, Leominster to Hereford, and Bridgnorth to Leintwardine via Corve Dale. He also considered possible links from Leintwardine to Hereford via Leominster and, alternatively, via Dilwyn and Canon Pyon; but time made a mockery of this enthusiasm. Those who subscribed to the Stourbridge-Leominster-Kington Canal project, authorized by Act in 1791, received neither interest nor capital repayment during the lifetime of the canal. When the Shrewsbury and Herefordshire Railway Company took over in 1858 the shareholders received £16 per £100 share. There were problems with Putnal tunnel, 320 metres long; and the 1143-metre Southnet tunnel collapsed. The latter was completed but no work was done on the proposed 3.5-kilometre Pensax tunnel or the ambitious flight of locks to lower the canal sixty-three metres to Stourport. West of Leominster there was only preparatory digging and aqueduct pier construction at Kingsland. North of Leominster its course is sometimes no more than a curving cropmark but the entrances to the Southnet and Putnal tunnels, and the Rea aqueduct, remain. The Teme aqueduct was demolished as an exercise in World War II. The Shrewsbury Canal was authorized in 1793 and opened in 1797. With the Shropshire Canal it linked Shrewsbury with the industrial area north of Coalbrookdale. Its 887-metre Berwick tunnel is an early example of a tunnel having a towpath; usually the boatmen had to leg it along the tunnel roof. Eleven locks were required to reach the earlier Wombridge Canal and the final ascent at Trench was achieved with a twenty-three metre climb up an inclined plane.

The imagination and skill of the canal engineers culminated in two outstanding monuments, the Chirk and Pont Cysyllte aqueducts. They were started to carry a projected Chester-Wrexham-Shrewsbury canal over the Ceiriog and Dee but a change of the main route left the canal from Lower Frankton to Llangollen as a branch of the Ellesmere Canal. Telford's Pont Cyssylte aqueduct is 307 metres long carrying a cast-iron trough supported by nineteen stone arches thirty-seven metres above the Dee. Opened in 1805, it is a fitting memorial to the canal era, daring in conception and thrilling in prospect. Three years earlier Coalbrookdale had built the world's first railway locomotives.

By 1833, when the Shropshire Union Canal was joined to the country's main network at Middlewich, the railways were poised to take over the markets sought by the canals. They tunnelled the Malverns and threw their splendid brick viaduct across the Leadon valley to link Hereford with the industrial Midlands. As they strove to thread branch lines through the hills to market towns of only 1500 or so, the illusion of riches to be won in the west evaporated. They joined the monuments of the Industrial Age that started in 1709 in Coalbrookdale.

There, in the Coalbrookdale Gorge Museum, we may inspect early blast furnaces and machinery, follow the line of early plateways and look upon chimney-pots, lamp-posts and window frames produced by the pioneers of cast-ironwork. About us is the industrial village that just about became a town, its church of 1854 and the Literary and Scientific Institute of 1859 built by ironmasters, whose houses stand close to the works beside the terraced cottages of the labour force.

Places to Visit

Museums Many of the finds are in Birmingham Museum, the British Museum, and the National Museum of Wales, Cardiff. Museums in the border itself include, from north to south, the Grosvenor in Chester, Rowley's House Shrewsbury, Wroxeter, Acton Scott Farm, Welshpool, Coalbrookdale and Blists Hill, Hartlebury, Clun, Ludlow, Leominster, Hereford, Abergavenny, Monmouth, Caerleon and Chepstow. The archaeological collections at Chester, Shrewsbury and Caerleon are especially important.

A short list of important sites normally open to the public

ACTON BURNELL Medieval fortified house 11 km SE of Shrewsbury. SJ 533 019
ARTHUR'S STONE Neolithic chamber tomb 9 km E of Hay-on-Wye. SO 318 432
BEESTON CASTLE Medieval castle 17km N of Whitchurch, Shropshire. SJ 537 592
BROCKHAMPTON MANOR Moated hall and gatehouse 3 km NE of Bromyard, SO 688 560
BURY DITCHES Multivallate hillfort 4 km S of Bishop's Castle. SO 327 835
CAER CARADOC Hillfort 3 km NE of Church Stretton. SO 478 953
CAERLEON Roman fortress barracks, baths and amphitheatre. ST 340 905
CAERWENT Roman town walls, temple and houses 6 km SW of Chepstow. ST 470 905
CHEPSTOW Norman castle, with later work, in Chepstow town. ST 533 941
CHESTER Roman fortress amphitheatre and medieval town walls. SJ 404 663
COALBROOKDALE Iron furnace and museum 6 km S of Wellington, Shropshire. SJ 669045
                Industrial monuments and machinery at Blists Hill, 3 km to E
COED Y BWNYDD Multivallate hillfort 6 km N of Usk. SO 365 068
CROFT AMBREY Multivallate hillfort reached from Croft Castle (below). SO 445 668
CROFT CASTLE Late medieval fortified house 9 km NW of Leominster. SO 450 654
DINEDOR CAMP Hillfort 4 km S of Hereford. SO 523 364
GOODRICH Castle with Norman keep and later work, 4 km SW of Ross. SO 577 199
HAROLD'S STONES Three prehistoric standing stones just SW of Trelleck. SO 499 050
HEREFORDSHIRE BEACON Hillfort with Norman ring-work 6 km NE of Ledbury. SO
                760400
LONGTOWN Castle and borough enclosure 15 km N of Abergavenny. SO 321 291
LUDLOW Castle with Norman and later work in town centre. SO 509 746
MIDSUMMER HILL CAMP Hillfort 5 km E of Ledbury. SO 760 374
MITCHELL'S FOLD Prehistoric stone circle 10 km N of Bishop's Castle. SO 304 984
MORETON CORBET Medieval fortified house 14 km NE of Shrewsbury. SJ 561 231
OLD OSWESTRY Multivallate hillfort 1 km N of Oswestry station. SJ 295 310
SKENFRITH Medieval castle 9 km NW of Monmouth. SO 457 202
STOKESAY CASTLE Medieval fortified manor 10 km NW of Ludlow. SO 436 817
SUDBROOK CAMP Multivallate coastal hillfort 6 km SW of Chepstow. ST 504 873
WAPLEY CAMP Multivallate hillfort 4 km SE of Presteigne. SO 346 623
WHITE CASTLE Norman castle with later work 8 km NE of Abergavenny. SO 380 168
WREKIN CAMP Multi-phase hillfort 4 km SW of Wellington, Shropshire. SJ 628 081
WROXETER Roman town with baths and forum colonnade 8 km SE of Shrewsbury SJ 560 088

BIBLIOGRAPHY

Maps   Consult the Ordnance Survey 1:50,000 sheets 117, 126, 127, 137, 138, 149, 162, and 171; and for local detail the relevant 1:25,000 sheets. The Ordnance Survey's period maps, particularly those of *Southern Britain during the Iron Age and Roman Britain*, will place the Marches in the wider context. The Geological Survey's regional handbooks *The Welsh Borderland, Central England, South Wales*, and *Bristol and Gloucester* are recommended.

Abbreviations: AC Archaeologia Cambrensis
AW See Council for British Archaeology, Archaeology in Wales
BBCS Bulletin of the Board of Celtic Studies
MA Medieval Archaeology   Mon Ant Monmouthshire Antiquary
PPS Proceedings Prehistoric Society
PSAL Proceedings Society Antiquaries London
RCHM Royal Commission on Historical Monuments
SN Shropshire Archaeological Society News Letter
TLCAS Transactions Lancashire & Cheshire Antiquarian Society
TSAS Transactions Shropshire Archaeological Society
TWNFC Transactions Woolhope Naturalists' Field Club
TWAS Transactions Worcestershire Archaeological Society

ABERG, F.A.(Ed) 1978. Medieval Moated Sites.
ALCOCK,L. et al 1968. ... Castell Bryn Amlwg. Montgomeryshire Collect. 60, 8-27
ALLEN, J.R.L. 1988. Reclamation and sea defence in Rumney parish.. AC 137, 135-40
ANDREWS, D.D. 1987. Shackerley Mound: a medieval moated site....TSAS 65, 12-32
ANTHONY, I.E. 1958. The Iron Age Camp at Poston, Herefordshire
ARNOLD, C.J. 1990. The Archaeology of Montgomeryshire
ASHMORE, P.J. and F.M. 1973. Excavations at Abergavenny .... Mon Ant 3, 104-110
ATKINSON,D. 1942. Report on excavations at Wroxeter 1923-1927
BABBIDGE, A. 1979. Reconnaissance excavations at Coed y Bwnydd.... Mon Ant 3, 159-78
BAGNALL-OAKLEY,M.E. 1889. Rude Stone Monuments in Monmouthshire
BAKER, A. 1968. Viroconium: a study of the defences.... TSAS 58, 197-219
BAKER, A. 1970a. Results in Herefordshire from aerial reconnaissance... TWNFC 40, 45-48
BAKER, A. 1970b. Aerial reconnaissance over Viroconium.... TSAS 59, 24-31
BARKER, P.A. 1959. The excavation of an enclosure at Uppington, Salop. TSAS 56,158-63
BARKER, P.A. 1961a. Excavations on the Town Wall, Roushill, Shrewsbury. MA 5, 181-210
BARKER, P.A. 1961b. A pottery sequence from Brockhurst Castle.... TSAS 57, 63-80
BARKER, P.A. 1964. Pontesbury Castle Mound Emergency Excavations.... TSAS 57, 206-23
BARKER, P.A. 1966. The deserted medieval hamlet of Braggington. TSAS 58, 122-39
BARKER, P.A. 1970. The medieval pottery of Shropshire from the Conquest to 1400.
BARKER, P.A. 1975. ... the baths basilica at Wroxeter, 1966-74 ... Britannia 6, 106-17
BARKER, P.A. *et al* 1991. Excavations on Sharpstones Hill.... TSAS 67, 15-57
BARLEY, M.W. (Ed) 1975. The plans and topography of medieval towns in England &Wales
BARNETT,C. 1961. A find of Roman pottery at Uskmouth. Mon Ant 1, 12-13.
BERESFORD, M.W. 1967. New Towns of the Middle Ages
BICK, D. 1984. Lime-kilns on the Gloucester'-Hereford' border. Ind Arch Rev 7, 85-93
BIRLEY, E., DOBSON,B., and JARRETT,M. (Eds) 1974. Roman Frontier Studies
BLAKE, J.E.H. 1913. ... Bronze Age at Mathon. T Proc Birmingham Archaeol Soc. 39, 90-3

BOON, G.C. 1987. The legionary fortress of Caerleon-Isca: a brief account
BOON, G.C. and LEWIS, J.M.T. (Eds) 1976. Welsh Antiquity
BRIDGEWATER, N.P. 1959a. The Whitchurch Vagas. TWNFC 36, 228-33
BRIDGEWATER, N.P. 1959b. Ancient buried roads in south Herefordshire. TWNFC 36,218-27
BRIDGEWATER, N.P. 1962. The Huntsham Romano-British Villa - First rep. TWNFC 37, 179-91
BRIDGEWATER, N.P. 1963. Glasshouse Farm, St Weonards .... TWNFC 37, 300-15
BRIDGEWATER, N.P. 1965. Romano-British iron working near Ariconium. TWNFC 38, 124-35
BRIDGEWATER, N.P. 1970. The Medieval Homestead of Wallingstones. TWNFC 40, 75-116
BRIGGS, S. 1977. Stone axe trade or glacial erratics? Current Archaeology 57, 303
BRITNELL, W. 1982. The .... Two Round Barrows at Trelystan, Powys. PPS 48, 133—201
BRITNELL, W. 1984. A Barbed Point from Porth-y-Waen, Llanyblodwel ...PPS 50, 385-6
BROWN, A.E. 1961. Records of surface finds in Herefordshire. TWNFC 37, 77-91
BROWN, R.ALLEN. 1976. English Castles (3rd edition)
BRYANT, A. 1835. Map of Herefordshire
BU'LOCK, J.D. 1956. The hill-fort at Helsby, Cheshire. TLCAS 66, 107-12
BU'LOCK, J.D. 1960. The Celtic, Saxon and Scandinavian settlement at Meols in Wirral. Trans Hist Soc Lancashire Cheshire. 112, 1-28
BURGESS, C.B. 1962. A socketed axe from central Monmouthshire... Mon Ant 1, 17-27
BURGESS, C. 1974. The Bronze Age. In RENFREW (Ed) British Prehistory,165-232
BURGESS, C. et al 1972. The Broadward Hoard ... In LYNCH & BURGESS (Eds) 211-84
BURGESS, C.B. & COWEN, J.D. 1972. The Ebnal Hoard .... In LYNCH & BURGESS (Eds) 167-82
BURNHAM, B.C. & DAVIES, J.L. (Eds) 1990. Conquest, Co-existence and Change. Trivium 25
BURNHAM, C.P. 1964. The soils of Herefordshire. TWNFC 38, 27-35
BURTON, J.R. 1890. History of Kidderminster
BUTLER, L.A.S. 1960. Excavations at Black Friars, Hereford, 1958. TWNFC 36, 334-62
BUTLER, L.A.S. 1965. St Kynemark's Priory, Chepstow. Mon Ant 2, 33-41
CARVER, M.O. 1974. Early Shrewsbury: an archaeological definition.... TSAS 59. 225-63
CASEY, P.J. et al 1983. Caerwent ... north-west corner tower... AC 132, 49-77
CASEY, P.J. 1989. Coin Evidence and the end of Roman Wales. Archaeol J 146, 320-329
CBA: See COUNCIL FOR BRITISH ARCHAEOLOGY
CHAPLIN, R.E. 1969. A forgotten industrial valley. Shropshire News Letter 36, 1-6
CHITTY, G. & WARHURST, M. 1977.Ancient Meols... J Merseyside Archaeol Soc 1, 19-42
CHITTY, L.F. 1925. Three bronze implements from .... Meole Brace. Antiq. J. 5, 109-14
CHITTY, L.F. 1926a. Notes on prehistoric implements. TSAS 43, 233-46
CHITTY, L.F. 1926b. The Hoar Stone or Marsh Pool Circle. TSAS 43, 247-53
CHITTY, L.F. 1927a. Bronze implements found near Castle Bryn Amlwg.... TSAS 44, v-vii
CHITTY, L.F. 1927b. Dug-out canoes from Shropshire. TSAS 44, 113-33
CHITTY, L.F. 1928. The Willow Moor Bronze Hoard, Little Wenlock ....Antiq. J. 8, 30-47
CHITTY, L.F. 1929. Notes on recent acquisitions .... Shrewsbury Museum. TSAS 45, 61-74
CHITTY, L.F. 1947. Report on bronze implements....at Netherwood.... TWNFC 32, xlv-xlix
CHITTY, L.F. 1949. Subsidiary Castle Sites West of Shrewsbury. TSAS 53, 86-90
CHITTY, L.F. 1963. The Clun-Clee Ridgeway .... In FOSTER & ALCOCK (Eds) 171-92
CLARK, G.T. 1884. Medieval Military Architecture
CLARK, R.M. 1975. A calibration curve for radio-carbon dates. Antiquity 49, 251-66
CLARK, S. et al 1985. Post-med'l potteries .... Medieval Later Pottery Wales 8,49-63
CLARK, S.C. et al 1982. Medieval iron working at Trelech ... Mon Ant 4, 45-9
COHEN, I. 1954. Archaeological Report for 1954. TWNFC 34, 296-301
COHEN, I. 1957. The Leominster-Stourport Canal. TWNFC 35, 267-86
COHEN, I. 1959. The Herefordshire and Gloucestershire Canal. TWNFC 36, 167-79
COLEMAN, V.H. 1964. The Kington Railway. TWNFC 38, 16-26
COLVIN, H.M. (Ed) et al 1963. The History of the King's Works,I & II:The Middle Ages
COOPE, G.R. & LISTER, A.M. 1987. ...mammoth skeletons from Condover. Nature 330, 472-4

COUNCIL FOR BRITISH ARCHAEOLOGY 1971. Archaeological site index to radiocarbon Dates for Great Britain and Ireland (Compiler C.Lavell). Additions published to 1982.

COUNCIL FOR BRITISH ARCHAEOLOGY. Group 2 Annual newsletter Archaeology in Wales- AW

COUNCIL FOR BRITISH ARCHAEOLOGY. Group 8 West Midlands Archaeological News Sheet- WMANS

COURTNEY, P. et al 1989. Excavations in the .. precinct of Tintern Abbey. MA 33, 99-143

CRASTER, O.E. 1956. Tintern Abbey Gwent. (Official Guide)

CRASTER, O.E. 1967. Skenfrith Castle: When was it built? AC 116, 333-58

CRASTER, O.E. & LEWIS, J.M. 1963. Hen Gwrt moated site.... AC 112, 159-83

CURNOW, P.E. 1989. The Tower House at Hopton Castle.... In HARPER-BILL, C. et al, Studies in medieval history presented to R. Allen Brown, 81-102

CURNOW, P.E. & JOHNSON, E.A. 1985. St Briavels Castle. Ch+teau Gaillard 12, 91-114

CURNOW, P.E. & THOMPSON, M.W. 1969. ...Richard's Castle.. J Brit Archaeol Ass 32, 105-27

DANIEL, D. 1950. Prehistoric Chamber Tombs of England and Wales

DARVILL, T. & STAELENS, Y. 1985. A 'Cumbrian' ... axe from Shropshire. BBCS 32,260-7

DAVEY, P.J. & FORSTER, E. 1975. Bronze Age Metalwork from Lancashire and Cheshire

DAVIES, W. 1979. Roman settlements and post-Roman estates in south-east Wales. In Casey, P.J.(Ed) The End of Roman Britain

DAVISON, B.K. 1969. Early earthwork castles: a new model. In TAYLOR (Ed) 45-6

DUKE, T.F. 1844. Antiquities of Shropshire from an old manuscript of Edward Lloyd...

EKWALL, E. 1960. The concise Oxford dictionary of English place-names (4th edition)

EMERY, A. 1975. The development of Raglan castle ..... Archaeol J 132, 151-86

EVANS, D.H. et al 1984. Further excavation .... Llanthony Priory ... Mon Ant 5,1-61

EVANS, SIR JOHN. 1881. Ancient Bronze Implements of Great Britain

FORDE-JOHNSTON, J. 1962. The Hillforts of Lancashire and Cheshire. TLCAS 72, 9-46

FORDE-JOHNSTON, J. 1976. Hilforts of the Iron Age in England and Wales

FOSTER, I.L. & ALCOCK, L. (Eds) 1963. Culture and Environment

FOWLER, P.J. (Ed). 1975. Recent work in rural archaeology

FOX, SIR CYRIL. 1952. The Personality of Britain (4th edition)

FOX, SIR CYRIL. 1955. Offa's Dyke

FRERE, S.S. 1987. Brandon Camp, Herefordshire. Britannia 18, 49-92

GAVIN-ROBINSON, R.S. 1954. Prehistoric Man in Herefordshire. In WOOLHOPE CLUB 107-19

GAYDON, A.T. (Ed) 1968. Victoria History of Shropshire - Vol. viii.

GELLING, M. 1978. Signposts to the Past

GELLING, M. ((Ed) 1983. Offa's Dyke Reviewed by Frank Noble

GELLING, M. 1984. Place-Names in the Landscape

GELLING, P.S. 1963. Excavations at Caynham Camp ....Final Report. TSAS 57, 91-100

GELLING, P.S. & PEACOCK, D.P.S. 1966. The pottery from Caynham Camp. TSAS 58, 96-100

GREEN, S. 1989. Some .... discoveries from the Severn Estuary Levels. BBCS 36, 187-99

GRIMES, W.F. 1930. Holt, Denbighshire, the works depot.... Y Cymmrodor 41

GRIMES, W.F. 1939. The Excavation of Ty-isaf Long Cairn, Brecknockshire, PPS 5,119-42

GRIMES, W.F. 1951. The Prehistory of Wales

GRIMES, W.F. 1963. The stone circles .... of Wales. In FOSTER & ALCOCK (Eds) 93-153

GUILBERT, G.C. 1975a. Planned hillfort interiors. PPS 41, 203-21

GUILBERT, G.C. 1975b. Ratlinghope/Stitt Hill, Shropshire .... BBCS 26, 363-73

GUILBERT, G.C. 1976a. Moel y Gaer (Rhosesmor) 1972-1973 .... In HARDING (Ed) 303-17

GUILBERT, G.C. 1976b. Caer-din ring, Salop. AC 125, 165-9

HADFIELD, C. 1966. The canals of the West Midlands

HADFIELD, C. 1967. The canals of South Wales and the Border

HAMILTON, W.G. 1938. Bronze Age burial site, Mathon. TWNFC 24, 120-7

HARDEN, D.B. (Ed) 1956. Dark Age Britain

HARDING, D.W. (Ed) 1976. Hillforts: Later Prehistoric Earthworks in Britain and Ireland

HARRIS, B.E. (Ed) 1987. A history of the county of Cheshire. Volume 1...

HEWITT, P.B. 1987. The Moated Site and ... village in ... Cleeton. TSAS 65, 33-7

HEYS, F.G. 1963. Excavations on a medieval site at Breinton.... TWNFC 37, 272-94

HEYS, F.G. & THOMAS, M. 1962. Excavations on.. defences of Kenchester. TWNFC 37, 149-78

HILL, D. 1974. The inter-relation of Offa's and Wat's Dykes. Antiquity 48, 309-12

HILL, D. 1981. Fieldwork notes on Offa's Dyke and others, in MA 184-5

HILLABY, J.G. 1970. The Boroughs of the Bishops of Hereford.... TWNFC 40,10-35

HILLABY, J.G. 1976. The origins of the diocese of Hereford. TWNFC 42, 16-52

HILLABY, J.G. & PEARSON, E.D. (Eds) 1970. Bromyard - A local history

HOGG, A.H.A. 1975. Hill-forts of Britain

HOGG, A.H.A. & KING, D.J.C. 1963. Early castles in Wales .... AC 112, 77-124

HOGG, A.H.A. & KING, D.J.C. 1967. Masonry castles in Wales .... AC 116, 71-132

HOGG, A.H.A. & KING, D.J.C. 1970. Castles in Wales ...Additions... AC 119, 119-24

HOPE, W.H.ST.JOHN, 1908. The Castle of Ludlow. Archaeologia 61, 257-328

HOPE, W.H.ST.JOHN, 1909. The ancient topography of ... Ludlow. Archaeologia 61,383-88

HOPE, W.H.ST.JOHN & BRAKSPEAR, H. 1909. Haughmond Abbey.... Archaeol J 66, 281-310

HOUGHTON, A.W.J. 1958. A note on .... the Roman villa at Lea Cross. TSAS 56, 26-7

HOUGHTON, A.W.J. 1960. The Roman Road from Greensforge .... TSAS 56, 233-43

HUME, C.R. & JONES,G.W. 1959. Excavations on Nesscliff Hill. TSAS 56, 129-32

IRON, D. 1953. Excavations at Clifford Castle during 1953. TWNFC 34, 82-4

JACK, G.H. 1924. Excavations on the site of Ariconium

JACK, G.H. & HAYTER, A.G.K. 1924. Excavations on the site of Caplar Camp. TWNFC83-8

JACK, G.H. & HAYTER, A.G.K. 1926. Excavations on the site of .... Kenchester, Vol II

JARRETT, M.G. (Ed) 1969. The Roman Frontier in Wales

JONES, G.B.D. 1979. Aerial Photography in N. Wales 1976-7. Aerial Photography 4,58-64

JONES, G.B.D. 1990. Searching for Caradog. In BURNHAM & DAVIES 1990, 57-64

JONES, G.B.D. & WEBSTER, P.V. 1968. Mediolanum... Whitchurch. Archaeol J 125, 193-254

JONES, H.C. 1936. A prehistoric burial in Clun Valley. Caradoc Trans 10. 74-80

JONES, H.C. 1940. Archaeological notes from the Clun Valley. Caradoc Trans 11, 126-31

JOPE, E.M. (Ed) 1961. Studies in building history.

JOPE, E.M. 1986. High precision radio-carbon dating. Antiq. J. 66, 358-60

KENYON, J.R. 1983. The Civil War earthworks around Raglan Castle ... AC 131, 139-42

KENYON, K.M. 1942. Excavations at the Wrekin, Shropshire. Archaeol J 99, 99-109

KENYON, K.M. 1954. Excavations at Sutton Walls. Archaeol J 110, 1-87

KING, D.J.C. & PERKS, J.C. 1956. Llangibby Castle. AC 105, 96-132

KING, D.J.C. & SPURGEON, C.J. 1965. The Mottes in the Vale of Montgomery. AC 114, 69-85

LEACH, G.B. 1960. Excavations at Hen Blas .... Trans Flints Hist Soc 18, 13-60

LEACH, P.J. 1971. Hereford Castle excavations 1968-69. TWNFC 40, 211-24

LEWIS, M.J.T. 1966. Temples in Roman Britain

LOBEL, M.D. (Ed) 1969. Historic Towns, Vol I

LOCKE, S. 1973. The post-glacial deposits of the Caldicot Level ... Mon Ant 3.1, 1-16

LYNCH, F. & BURGESS,C. (Eds) 1972. Prehistoric Man in Wales and the West

MANNING, W.H. 1981... Usk 1965-76. The fortress excavations 1968-71

MANNING, W.H. with SCOTT,I.R. 1989. Report on the excavations at Usk 1965-1976 ....

MARGARY, I.D. 1967. Roman roads in Britain

MARSHALL,G. 1930-2. .... two Bronze Age cists in the Olchon Valley. TWNFC 147-53

MARSHALL, G. 1946. Potteries in North Herefordshire. TWNFC (1946), 1-12

MARTIN, S.H. 1954. The chapel of St Dubric in Woolhope. TWNFC 34, 229-32

MASON, D.J.P. 1986. Chester: plan of the fortress....Britannia 17, 388

MASON, D.J.P. 1987. Chester: the Canabae Legionis. Britannia 18, 143-69

MASON, D.J.P. 1988. The Roman site at Heronbridge .... Archaeol J 145, 123-57

MORAN, M. 1989. Re-erecting houses in Shropshire .... Archaeol J 146, 538-553

MORGAN, F.C. 1956. Herefordshire Potteries. TWNFC 35, 133-8

MORRIS, E. 1985. Prehistoric salt distributions .... BBCS 32, 336-79

MORRIS, J. 1973. The age of Arthur: a history of the British Isles from 350-650

MORRIS, J.A. 1926. Excavations at Stowe, Shropshire. TSAS 10, iv

MUSSON, C. 1991. The Breiddin Hillfort: A later prehistoric settlement....

MUSSON, C.R.& SPURGEON, C.J. 1988. Cwrt Llechrhyd, Llanelwedd... MA 32, 97-109

MUTTON, N. 1965. Charlcotte Furnace. TSAS 58, 84-8

NASH-WILLIAMS, V.E. 1933. An Early Iron Age hill-fort at Llanmelin.... AC 88, 237-346
NASH-WILLIAMS, V.E. 1939. Early Iron Age .... camp at Sudbrook. AC 94, 42-79
NEAL, S.COOPER. 1927. An ancient cottage pottery in Upton Bishop. TWNFC 144-6, 207-8
NOBLE, F. 1964. Medieval Boroughs of West Herefordshire. TWNFC 38, 62-70
NORWOOD, J.N.L. 1957. Prehistoric accessions to Hereford Museum. TWNFC 35, 316-3
NORWOOD, J.N.L. 1963. Prehistoric accessions to Hereford Museum. TWNFC 37, 345-50.
O'NEIL, B.ST J. Usk Castle (Official Guide)
O'NEIL, B.ST J. 1934. Excavations at Titterstone Clee Camp, 1932. AC 89, 83-111
PAAR, H.W. & TUCKER, D.G. 1975. ..ironworks ... Angidy valley .. Hist Metall 9(1), 1-14
PALMER, A.N. 1907/8. History of Holt. Arch Camb 62, 311-4, 389-402; 63, 155-63
PEACOCK, D.P.S. 1967. Romano-British pottery ... Malvern district ... TWAS 1, 15-29
PEACOCK, D.P.S. 1968. .... Iron Age pottery from Western England. PPS 34, 414-27
PEACOCK, D.P.S. 1969. A .... study of Glastonbury ware. Antiq J 49, 41-61
PERKS, J.C. 1955. Chepstow Castle (Official Guide)
PHILLIPS, C.W. 1931. ....Merlin's Cave. Proc Univ Bristol Spelaeol Soc 4, 11-32
PICKIN, J. 1982 & 1983. ... Abbey Tintern Furnace. Hist Metall 16, 1-21; 17, 4-11
POWELL, T.G.E. 1966. Prehistoric Art
PRICE, F.G.H. 1880. Camps on the Malvern Hills. TWNFC (1880) 217-27
PROBERT, L.A. 1976. Twyn y Gaer hill-fort, Gwent .... In BOON & LEWIS (Eds) 105-14
RADCLIFFE, F. & KNIGHT,J. 1973. Excavations at Abergavenny .... Mon Ant 3, 65-103
RADFORD, C.A.R. 1946. Grosmont Castle (Official Guide)
RADFORD, C.A.R. 1958. The Medieval Defences of Shrewsbury. TSAS 56, 15-20
RADFORD, C.A.R. 1961. Acton Burnell Castle. In JOPE (Ed) 94-103
RADFORD, C.A.R. 1962. White Castle (Official Guide)
RENN, D.F. 1958. The Water Tower at Chester. J Chester and N.Wales AAHS 45, 56-60
RENN, D.F. 1961. The Round Keeps of the Brecon Region. AC 110, 129-43
RENNELL, LORD. 1970. A Roman road from Mortimer's Cross to Clyro... TWNFC 40, 36-44
RICHARDS, M. 1973. The 'Lichfield' gospels (Book of St Chad). Nat Libr Wales J 18
RICHMOND, I.A. 1963. The Cornovii. In FOSTER & ALCOCK (Eds) 251-62
RIDGEWAY, M.H. & KING, D.C.J. 1959. Beeston Castle. J Cheshire & N Wales AS 46,1-23
RIVET, A.L.F. & SMITH,C. 1979. The Place-Names of Roman Britain
ROBERTS, B.K. 1964. Moats and Mottes. MA 8, 219-22
RODWELL, W. & ROWLEY, T.(Eds) 1975. The small towns of Roman Britain
ROWLANDS, M.J. 1976. Middle Bronze Age metalworking
ROWLEY, T. 1972. The Shropshire Landscape
ROYAL COMMISSION ON HISTORICAL MONUMENTS. 1931 Herefordshire I - South-west.
            1932 Herefordshire II - East. 1934 Herefordshire III - North-west
RUSSELL, J.C. 1948. British Medieval Population
ST JOSEPH, J.K.S. 1951. Roman forts .... Penkridge and Wroxeter. T Birm AS 69, 53-6
ST JOSEPH, J.K.S. 1961. Aerial reconnaissance in Wales. Antiquity 35, 263-75
ST JOSEPH, J.K.S. 1965. Air reconnaissance in Britain, 1961-4. J Roman Stud 55,74-89
ST JOSEPH, J.K.S. 1973. Air reconnaissance in Roman Britain ... J Roman Stud 63, 214-46
ST JOSEPH, J.K.S. 1977. Air reconnaissance: recent results, 42. Antiquity 51, 55-60
SAUNDERS, A.D. 1977. Five castle excavations - introduction. Archaeol J 134, 1-10
SAVILLE, A. 1974. .. flint artifacts from .. south-east Shropshire ... TSAS 59,198-208
SAVORY, H.N. 1940. A Middle Bronze Age barrow at Crick .... AC 95, 169-91
SAVORY, H.N. 1948. A bronze socketed axe .... from Llanfair Cilgedyn. BBCS 13, 55-6
SAVORY, H.N. 1963. The Southern Marches .... In FOSTER & ALCOCK (Eds) 25-52
SHOESMITH, R. 1980. The Roman Buildings at New Weir, Herefordshire. TWNFC 43, 135-54
SHOESMITH, R. 1980 & 1982 Hereford City Excavations Vols 1 & 2
SHOTTON, F.W., et al 1951. A new centre of stone axe dispersal ... PPS 17, 159-67
SIMPSON, G. 1964. Britons and the Roman army
SMITH, R.A. 1907. The timekeepers of the Ancient Britons. PSAL 21, 319-34
STANFORD, S.C. 1959. ... the Roman Outpost at Clifton-on-Teme ....TWAS 36, 19-32
STANFORD, S.C. 1965. A medieval settlement at Detton Hall. TSAS 58, 27-47
STANFORD, S.C. 1967. The Deserted Medieval Village of Hampton Wafer ..TWNFC 39,71-92
STANFORD, S.C. 1968b. The Roman forts at Leintwardine and Buckton. TWNFC 39, 222-326

STANFORD, S.C. 1970. Credenhill Camp, Herefordshire. Archaeol J 127, 82-129

STANFORD, S.C. 1972a. Welsh Border Hill-forts. In THOMAS (Ed) 25-36

STANFORD, S.C. 1972b. The Function and Population of hill-forts in the central Marches. In LYNCH & BURGESS (Eds) 307-20

STANFORD, S.C. 1973. The Malvern Hill-forts

STANFORD, S.C. 1974a. Croft Ambrey

STANFORD, S.C. 1974b. Native and Roman .... borderland. In BIRLEY et al (Eds) 44-60.

STANFORD, S.C. (Ed) 1976. Guide to prehistoric and Roman sites in Herefordshire

STANFORD, S.C. 1981. Midsummer Hill, An Iron Age Hillfort on the Malverns

STANFORD, S.C. 1982. Bromfield .... Neolithic and Bronze Age sites. PPS 48, 279-320

STANFORD, S.C. 1984. The Wrekin Hillfort Excavations 1973. Archaeol J 141, 61-90

STANFORD, S.C. 1985a. Bromfield .... From Neolithic to Saxon times. TSAS 64, 1-7

STANFORD, S.C. 1985b. Ebury Hill Camp - Excavations 1977. TSAS 64, 9-16

STENTON, SIR FRANK (Ed). 1957. The Bayeux Tapestry

STUIVER, M & PEARSON, G.W. High precision calibration of the radiocarbon time scale AD 1950-500 BC. and (PEARSON & STUIVER) 500-2500 BC. Radiocarbon (1986), 805-862

SYLVESTER, D. & NULTY, G. (Eds). 1958. The historical atlas of Cheshire

SYMONDS, W.S. 1871. On the contents of a hyena's den on the Great Doward, Whitchurch, Ross. Geological Magazine 8, 433

TACITUS (Translated M.Grant 1956). Tacitus on Imperial Rome

TAYLOR, A.J. 1951. Monmouth Castle (Official Guide)

TAYLOR, A.J. 1961. White Castle in the thirteenth century .... MA 5, 169-75

TAYLOR, A.J. 1965. Chepstow Castle (Official Guide)

TAYLOR, A.J. (Ed) 1969. Ch+teau Gaillard European Castle Studies III

TAYLOR, E. 1986. The Seventeenth Century Iron Forge at Carey Mill. TWNFC 45, 450-68

TAYLOR, H. 1928. .... King Arthur's Cave. Proc Univ Bristol Spelaeol Soc 3, 59-83

TAYLOR, J. 1786. Map of Herefordshire

THOMAS, C. (Ed) 1966. Rural settlement in Roman Britain

THOMAS, N. 1972. An Early Bronze Age Stone-Axe-Mould .. In LYNCH & BURGESS (Eds) 161-66

THOMPSON, F.H. 1959. Deva - Roman Chester

THOMPSON, F.H. 1975. The .... Roman amphitheatre at Chester. Archaeologia 105, 1 27-240

TOMS, G.S.G. 1970. 2a St Alkmund's Place ....Shrewsbury. TSAS 59, 32-42

TRINDER, B. 1973. The Industrial Revolution in Shropshire

TYLER, A. 1984. The Burgs, Bayston Hill, Shropshire. BBCS 31, 203-8

VAN LAUN, J. 1979. ... ironmaking in south-west Herefordshire. Hist Metall 13, 55-68

VARLEY, W.J. 1935 & 1936. Maiden Castle, Bickerton .... Liverpool Univ Annals A & A 22, 97-110; 23, 101-12

VARLEY, W.J. 1948. The hill-forts of the Welsh Marches. Archaeol J 105, 41-60

VARLEY, W.J. 1950. ... Castle Ditch, Eddisbury, 1935-38. T H S Lancs & Chesh 102, 1-68

VARLEY, W.J., JACKSON, J.W. & CHITTY, L.F. 1940. Prehistoric Cheshire

VCH: VICTORIA COUNTY HISTORY 1908a. Shropshire.   1908b Herefordshire

VYNER, B.E. 1978.... Great Bulmore. In Cambrian Arch. Ass. Monographs & Collections I,25-31

WACHER, J. 1975a. The Towns of Roman Britain

WACHER, J. 1975b. Village fortifications. In RODWELL & ROWLEY (Eds) 51-2

WADDELOVE, 1984. The Location of Bovium. Britannia 15, 255-7

WADE-MARTINS, P. 1975. .... rural settlement in East Anglia. In FOWLER (Ed) 137-57

WALKER, C.I. 1965. Excavations at the Roman fort at Walltown Farm .... TSAS 58,8-18

WALLER, D. 1970. Lost Beginnings. In HILLABY & PEARSON (Eds) 5-6

WARG: See WOOLHOPE ARCHAEOLOGICAL RESEARCH GROUP NEWS-SHEET

WARRILOW, W. et al 1986. Eight ring-ditches at ... Llandysilio, Powys. PPS 52, 53-88

WATKINS, A. 1926. Excavations at the Queen Stone. TWNFC (1926) 189-93

WATSON, M.D. 1987. Gazetteer of Moated Sites in Shropshire. TSAS 65, 1-11

WEBSTER, G. 1953. ... Lead-mining ... in N.Wales ... Trans Flintshire Hist Soc 13, 3-31

WEBSTER, G. 1954. The Roman Fort at Tedstone Wafer. TWNFC 34, 284-7

WEBSTER, G. 1956. An .... earthwork at Linley Hill, More. TSAS 55, 119-21

WEBSTER, G. 1981. Rome Against Caratacus

WEBSTER, G. 1975. The Cornovii
WEBSTER, G. 1987. Wroxeter. Curr Archaeol 9, 364-8
WHEELER, R.E.M. & T.V. 1928. ... amphitheatre at Caerleon... Archaeologia 78, 111-218.
WHEELER, R.E.M. 1932. The .... Prehistoric, Roman and post-Roman site in Lydney Park
WHITTLE, A.W.R. et al 1989. Two Later Bronze Age occupations...Gwent... BBCS 36, 200-23
WILMOTT, A.R. 1980. Kenchester (Magnis): a reconsideration. TWNFC 43, 117-34
WILMOTT, A.R. & RAHTZ, S.P.Q. 1985. .. settlement outside Kenchester. TWNFC 45,36-185
WILSON. D. 1987. The ... moated sites of Cheshire. Tr Lancs Chesh Ant Soc 84, 143-54
WILSON, D.R. 1968. Roman Britain in 1967. J Roman Stud 58, 176-206
WILSON, D.R. 1984. The plan of Viroconium Cornoviorum. Antiquity 223, 117-20
WMANS: See COUNCIL FOR BRITISH ARCHAEOLOGY. West Midlands Archaeological
                                                                      News Sheet
WOOD, M.E. 1950. Thirteenth-century domestic architecture ... Archaeol J 105, Sup. 64-9
WOODS, H. 1987. Excavations at Wenlock Priory ... J Brit Archaeol Ass 140, 36-75
WOOLHOPE CLUB. 1954. Herefordshire
WOOLHOPE ARCHAEOLOGICAL RESEARCH GROUP NEWS-SHEET (Abbr. WARG)
WRAY, A. (1805-74) Metalwork of the Bronze Age, Vol 2. Soc of Antiq of London Library
WRIGHT, C.F. 1964. Craswall Priory .... field study made in 1962. TWNFC 38, 76-81
WRIGHT, T. 1872. Uriconium
WRIGHT, R.P. & JACKSON, K.H. 1968. .... inscription from Wroxeter. Antiq J. 48,296-300
ZIENKIEWICZ, J.D. 1986. The legionary fortress baths at Caerleon. Vols 1 & 2
ZIENKIEWICZ, J.D. 1990. The early .. ... Caerleon .. In BURNHAM & DAVIES (Eds),27-34

Index

Numbers in italics denote pages on which drawings or photographs appear